GUITAR CHORD SONGBOOK

TOP 100

prAise & wOrsHip

songbook

BRENTWOOD-BENSON®
music publishing

www.brentwoodbenson.com

MMVI Brentwood-Benson Music Publishing, 741 Cool Springs Blvd., Franklin, TN 37067.
All Rights Reserved. Unauthorized Duplication Prohibited.

Above All

Words and Music by
PAUL BALOCHE
and LENNY LEBLANC

Melody:

A - bove all__ pow - ers,

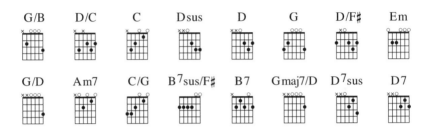

Verse

$\quad$ **G/B** $\quad$ **D/C** **C** **Dsus** **D** $\quad$ **G**
Above all pow- ers, $\quad$ above all kings,

G/B $\qquad$ **D/C** **C** $\qquad$ **Dsus** **D** **G**
$\quad$ Above all na- $\quad$ ture and all $\;$ created things;

D/F♯ $\quad$ **Em** $\qquad$ **G/D** $\qquad$ **C** **G/B**
Above all wisdom and all the ways of man,

Am7 $\qquad$ **C/G** $\qquad$ **D/F♯**
You were here before the world began.

G **G/B** $\;$ **D/C** **C** $\quad$ **Dsus** **D** $\quad$ **G**
$\quad$ Above all king- doms, $\quad$ above all thrones,

G/B $\qquad$ **D/C** **C** $\qquad$ **Dsus** $\quad$ **D** **G**
$\quad$ Above all won- $\quad$ ders the world has ever known;

D/F♯ $\quad$ **Em** $\qquad$ **G/D** $\qquad$ **C** **G/B**
Above all wealth and treasures of the earth,

Am7 $\qquad$ **C/G** $\qquad\qquad$ **B7sus/F♯** **B7**
There's no way to measure what You're worth.

Chorus   **G**   **Am7** **D/F♯**   **G**
Crucified,   laid behind the stone;
            Am7 **D/F♯**   **G**
You lived to die,   rejected and alone;
D/F♯ **Em** **Gmaj7/D**   **C** **G/B**
Like a rose, trampled on the ground
            Am7 **G/B**
You took the fall
            C **D7sus** **D7** **G**
And thought of me   above all.

Alive, Forever, Amen

Words and Music by
TRAVIS COTTRELL,
DAVID MOFFITT
and SUE C. SMITH

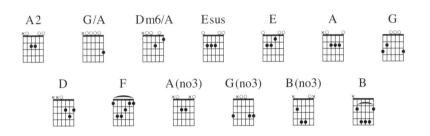

Verse 1

  A2   **G/A**
  Let the children sing   a song of liberation.
  Dm6/A   **A2**
  The God of our salvation set us free.
                    G/A
  Death where is thy sting?   The curse of sin is broken;
  Dm6/A   **Esus**   **E**
  The empty tomb stands open. Come and see.

Chorus

    A   **G**   **D**
  He's alive, alive, alive. Hallelujah, alive.
        F   **G**   **A**
  Praise and glory to the Lamb.
    A   **G**   **D**   **F** **G** **A**
  Alive, alive, alive. Hallelujah. Alive forever. A- men.

Verse 2   **A2**
    Let my heart sing out,
G/A
    For Christ, the One and only,
Dm6/A   **A2**
    So powerful and holy, rescued me.

    Death won't hurt me now
G/A
    Because He has redeemed me.
Dm6/A   **Esus**   **E**
    No grave will ever keep me from my King.

Bridge   **A(no3)**
    Worthy is the Lamb, worthy of our praise.
G(no3)
    Worthy is the One who has overcome the grave.
D   **F**   **G**
    Let the people dance; let the people sing.
A(no3)
    Worthy is the mighty King.

Bridge   **B(no3)**
(in B)
    Worthy is the Lamb, worthy of our praise.
A(no3)
    Worthy is the One who has overcome the grave.
E   **G**   **A**
    Let the people dance; let the people sing.
B(no3)
    Worthy is the mighty King.

Tag   **A2**   **B**   **A2** **A** **B**
    You are worthy.   A- men!

Ancient of Days

Words and Music by
JAMIE HARVILL
and GARY SADLER

C   Dm/C   Csus   G/B   Am

Am7   F   Dm7   G   C/E

Em7   Cmaj7/E   B♭/C   F/C   Gm/C

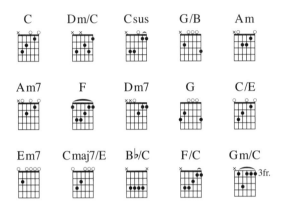

Verse

C	**Dm/C**	**C**	**Dm/C**	**C**

Blessing and honor, glory and power

Csus C G/B Am G/B

Be unto the Ancient of   Days.

C   Dm/C C   Dm/C C

From every   nation, all of crea-   tion,

Am7   G/B C

Bow before the Ancient of   Days.

Chorus   **F**   **Dm7**   **G**   **C/E**
Every tongue in heaven and earth shall declare Your glory.
F   **Dm7**   **G**   **C/E**   **Em7**
Every knee shall bow at Your throne in wor-   ship.
F   **Dm7**   **G**
You will be exalted, O God,
C/E   **Cmaj7/E** **F**   **Dm7**   **G**
And   Your   kingdom shall not pass away,
           C **Csus** **C**
O Ancient of Days.

Bridge   **C**   **Dm/C** **C**   **Dm/C** **C**
Your kingdom shall   reign over   all the earth;
B♭/C **F/C** **Gm/C**   **B♭/C**   **C**
Sing unto the An-   cient of Days!
            Dm/C **C**   **Dm/C** **C**
For none can com-   pare to Your   matchless worth;
B♭/C **F/C** **Gm/C**   **B♭/C**   **C**   **C/E**
Sing unto the An-   cient of Days!

As the Deer

Words and Music by
MARTIN NYSTROM

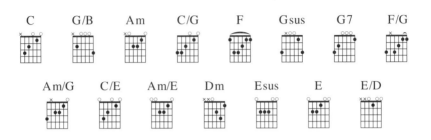

Verse 1
C   G/B   Am   C/G
As the deer panteth for the water,
         F   Gsus G7 C F/G G7
So my soul longeth af-   ter Thee.
C   G/B   Am   C/G
You alone are my heart's desire
         F   Gsus G7   C   G/B
And I long to wor-   ship Thee.

Chorus
Am Am/G   F   C/E
You alone are my strength, my shield;
        F   Am/E   Dm Esus E E/D
To You alone may my spirit yield.
C   G/B   Am   C/G
You alone are my heart's desire
         F   Gsus G7   C
And I long to wor-   ship Thee.

Verse 2   C   G/B   Am   C/G
You're my friend and You are my brother,
        F   Gsus G7 C F/G G7
Even though You are   a King.
C   G/B   Am   C/G
I love You more than any   other,
       F   Gsus G7 C G/B
So much more than an-   ything.

Verse 3   C   G/B   Am   C/G
I want You more than gold or silver,
       F   Gsus G7 C F/G G7
Only You can sat-   isfy.
C   G/B   Am   C/G
You alone are the real joygiver,
       F   Gsus G7   C G/B
And the apple of   my eye.

Agnus Dei

Words and Music by
MICHAEL W. SMITH

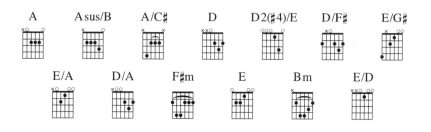

Verse
A Asus/B A/C♯ D A/C♯
Al-   le-   lu- ia,
A Asus/B A/C♯ D D2(♯4)/E D/F♯
Al-   le-   lu-   ia,
     D2(♯4)/E   D   A/C♯ A
For the Lord God Almighty reigns.   *(Repeat)*
A Asus/B A/C♯ D D2(♯4)/E D/F♯
Al-   le-   lu-   ia!

Chorus
D/F♯ E/G♯ A
Ho-   ly,
E/A A   D/A A   F♯m E
Ho- ly are You, Lord God Almight- y.
Bm   A/C♯ D   Bm   A/C♯   D
Worthy is   the Lamb, worthy is   the Lamb,
      E/D D E/D A
You are   ho-   ly,
E/A A   D/A A   F♯m E
Ho- ly are You, Lord God Almight- y.
Bm   A/C♯ D   Bm   A/C♯   D   E A
Worthy is   the Lamb, worthy is   the Lamb, A-   men!

Awesome God

Words and Music by
RICH MULLINS

Melody:

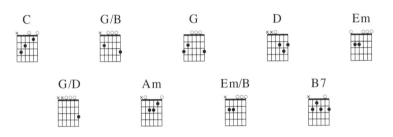

Our God is an awe-some God.

C   G/B   G   D   Em

G/D   Am   Em/B   B7

Chorus
        C   **G/B**   **G**
Our God is an awesome God.
     D   **Em**
He reigns from heaven above
G/D **C**   **G/B**   **G**
With   wisdom, pow'r and love.
     Am   **Em/B** **B7** **Em**
Our God is an awe-   some God!

Awesome in this Place

Words and Music by
DAVE BILLINGTON

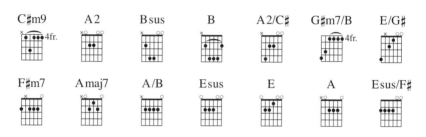

As I come in-to——Your pres - ence,

C♯m9	A2	Bsus	B	A2/C♯	G♯m7/B	E/G♯

F♯m7	Amaj7	A/B	Esus	E	A	Esus/F♯

Verse

  C♯m9   A2
As I come into Your presence, past the gates of praise,
  C♯m9   A2
Into Your sanctuary 'til we're standing face to face.
 Bsus   B
I look upon Your countenance,
   A2/C♯ G♯m7/B A2 E/G♯
I see the fullness of   Your grace.
   F♯m7 E/G♯ Amaj7 Bsus B
And I can only bow down and   say,

Chorus A/B Esus   E   F♯m7 E/G♯
You are awesome in this place, Mighty God.
        A   A/B   E   A/B
You are awesome in this place, Abba Father.
       E   Esus/F♯ E/G♯ A2   E/G♯   F♯m7
You are worthy of   all praise, to You our lives we raise.
       A/B   E
You are awesome in this place, Mighty God.

Be Glorified

Words and Music by
LOUIE GIGLIO,
JESSE REEVES,
and CHRIS TOMLIN

Melody:

Your love— has cap - tured— me,—

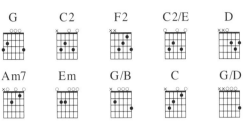

| G | C2 | F2 | C2/E | D |
| Am7 | Em | G/B | C | G/D |

Verse   G   C2   F2   C2/E
       Your love has captured me,
G   C2   D
       Your grace has set me free;
G   C2   F2   C2/E   Am7   D   G   C2
       Your life, the air I breathe.   Be glorified in me.
F2   C2/E   G   C2   F2   C2/E

Chorus   C2   G
       You set my feet to dancing,   You set my heart on fire.
      C2   G
In the presence of a thousand kings, You are my one desire.
      C2
       And I stand before You now
      Em   D   C2
With trembling hands lifted high.
        G   C2   F2   C2/E   G   C2   F2   C2/E   (G)
Be glorified.

Bridge   G/B   C   D   G/D G/B   C   D
       Be glo-   rified in me, be glo-   rified in me,
     G/D   G/B   C   D   G/D   G/B   C
       Be glo-   rified in me, be glo-   rified.

Be Unto Your Name

Words and Music by
LYNN DeSHAZO
and GARY SADLER

Melody:

We are a mo - ment, ___

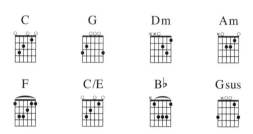

Verse 1
   C   **G**   **Dm**   **Am**
We are a moment, You are forever,
F   **C/E** **B♭**   **Gsus** **G**
Lord of the ages, God before time.
C   **G**   **Dm**   **Am**
We are a vapor, You are eternal,
F   **C/E** **B♭**   **Gsus** **G**
Love everlasting, reigning on high.

Chorus   **Am F C/E   G**
Holy, holy, Lord God Almighty.
Am F C   Gsus G
Worthy is the Lamb who was slain.
Am F C/E   G
Highest praises, honor and glory
Dm   Am   Gsus G
    Be unto Your name,
Dm   Am   Gsus G C
    Be unto Your name.

Verse 2   **C   G   Dm   Am**
We are the broken, You are the healer,
F   C/E B♭   Gsus G
Jesus, Redeemer, mighty to save.
C   G   Dm   Am
You are the love song we'll sing forever,
F   C/E B♭   Gsus G
Bowing before You, blessing Your name.

Better Is One Day

Words and Music by
MATT REDMAN

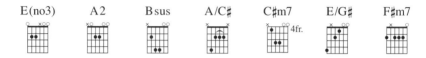

E(no3) A2 B sus A/C♯ C♯m7 E/G♯ F♯m7

Verse 1

    E(no3)   **A2**   **Bsus**
How lovely is Your dwelling place,   O Lord almighty.
    E(no3)   **Bsus**
For my soul longs and even faints for You.
    E(no3)   **A2**   **Bsus**
For here my heart is satisfied   within Your presence.
    E(no3)   **Bsus**
I sing beneath the shadow of Your wings.

Chorus

    A2
Better is one day in Your courts,
    Bsus
Better is one day in Your house,
    A2   **A/C♯**   **Bsus**
Better is one day in Your courts than thousands elsewhere.
    A2
Better is one day in Your courts,
    Bsus
Better is one day in Your house,
    A2   **A/C♯**   **Bsus**
Better is one day in Your courts than thousands elsewhere,
    E(no3)
Than thousands elsewhere.

Verse 2   **E(no3)**   **A2**   **Bsus**
One thing I ask, and I would seek: to see Your beauty,
      E(no3)   **Bsus**
To find You in the place Your glory dwells.
      E(no3)   **A2**   **Bsus**
One thing I ask, and I would seek: to see Your beauty,
      E(no3)   **Bsus**
To find You in the place Your glory dwells.

Bridge   **C♯m7**   **Bsus**
      My heart and flesh cry out
A2   **Bsus**
      For You, the living God.
C♯m7   **Bsus A2 Bsus**
      Your Spirit's water to my soul.
C♯m7   **Bsus**
      I've tasted and I've seen.
A2
      Come once again to me.
E/G♯
      I will draw near to You,
F♯m7   **Bsus**
      I will draw near to You, to You.

Blessed Be Your Name

Words and Music by
MATT REDMAN
and BETH REDMAN

Verse 1

    A   **E**   **F♯m7**   **D2**
Blessed be Your name in the land that is plentiful,
         A   **E**
Where Your streams of abundance flow;
     D2
Blessed be Your name.
    A   **E**   **F♯m7**   **D2**
Blessed be Your name when I'm found in the desert place,
     A   **E**   **D2**
When I walk through the wilderness; blessed be Your name.

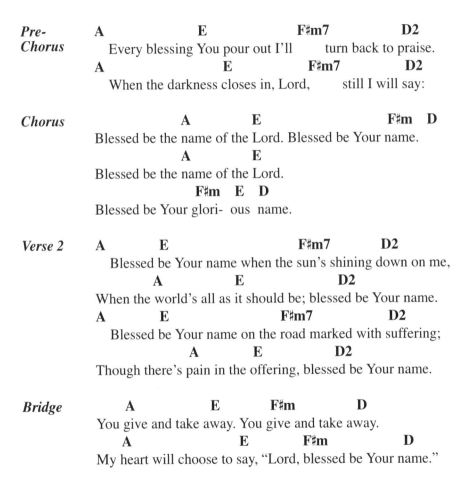

Pre-
Chorus

  A   E   F♯m7   D2
Every blessing You pour out I'll   turn back to praise.
A   E   F♯m7   D2
When the darkness closes in, Lord,   still I will say:

Chorus

                A   E   F♯m D
Blessed be the name of the Lord. Blessed be Your name.
                A   E
Blessed be the name of the Lord.
                F♯m E D
Blessed be Your glori- ous name.

Verse 2

  A   E   F♯m7   D2
Blessed be Your name when the sun's shining down on me,
              A   E   D2
When the world's all as it should be; blessed be Your name.
A   E   F♯m7   D2
Blessed be Your name on the road marked with suffering;
              A   E   D2
Though there's pain in the offering, blessed be Your name.

Bridge

      A   E   F♯m   D
You give and take away. You give and take away.
      A   E   F♯m   D
My heart will choose to say, "Lord, blessed be Your name."

Beautiful One

Words and Music by
TIM HUGHES

Won - der - ful,   so   won - der - ful,

G	A	D/F♯	Bm7	D

Verse 1   **G**   **A**   **D/F♯**
Wonderful, so wonderful, is Your unfailing love.
　　　　　　G   **A**   **Bm7**
Your cross has spoken mercy over me.
　　　　　　G   **A**   **D/F♯**
No eye has seen, no ear has heard, no heart could fully know
　　　　　　G   **A**   **D**
How glorious, how beautiful You are.

Chorus   **G**   **A**   **G**   **A**
Beautiful One I love, beautiful One I adore,
　　　　　　G   **A**   **D**
Beautiful One, my soul must sing.

Verse 2   **G**   **A**   **D/F♯**
Powerful, so powerful, Your glory fills the skies,
　　　　　　G   **A**   **Bm7**
Your mighty works displayed for all to see.
　　　　　　G   **A**   **D/F♯**
The beauty of Your majesty awakes my heart to sing.
　　　　　　G   **A**   **D**
How marvelous, how wonderful You are.

Bridge   **G**   **A**
You opened my eyes to Your wonders anew.
　　　　　　G   **A**
You captured my heart with this love,
　　　　　　G   **A**   **D**
'Cause nothing on earth is as beautiful as You.

Breathe

Words and Music by
MARIE BARNETT

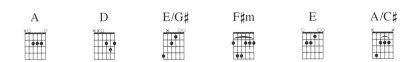

This is —— the air —— I breathe,

A   D   E/G♯   F♯m   E   A/C♯

Verse

A   D   A   D
This is the air I breathe,   this is the air I breathe,
A   E/G♯   F♯m   E   D   A/C♯   E
Your holy   presence   living   in me.
A   D   A   D
This is my daily bread,   this is my daily bread,
A   E/G♯   F♯m   E   D   A/C♯   E
Your very   Word   spoken   to me.

Chorus

   A   E/G♯   F♯m   E   D   F♯m   E
And I,   I'm desp'rate for You.
   A   E/G♯   F♯m   E   D   F♯m   E   (A)
And I,   I'm lost without You.

Come Just As You Are

Words and Music by
JOSEPH SABOLICK

Come just as you are;

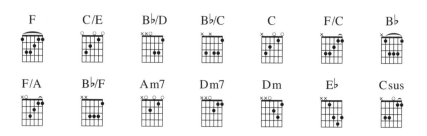

Chorus 1   F   C/E   Bb/D   Bb/C   C
Come just as you are;
F   C/E   Bb/D   Bb/C   C
Hear the Spirit call.
F   C/E   Bb/D   F/C
Come just as you are;
Bb   F/A   Bb   F/C   C
Come and see, come receive; Come and live forev-   er.

Verse   Bb   Bb/F   F   Am7   Dm7
Life everlast- ing,
       Bb   F   Dm   C
And strength for today;
Bb   Bb/F   F   Dm7   Eb   Bb/D   Csus   C
Taste the Living Wa-   ter,   and never thirst again.

Chorus 2   **F**   **C/E**   **B♭/D**   **B♭/C**   **C**
Come just as you are;
F   **C/E**   **B♭/D**   **B♭/C**   **C**
Hear the Spirit call.
F   **C/E**   **B♭/D**   **F/C**
Come just as you are;
B♭   **F/A**   **B♭**   **F/C**   **C**
Come, receive Christ, the King; Come and live forever.

Tag   **B♭**   **F/C**   **C**   **F**
(last time) Come and live forev-   er- more.

Change My Heart, O God

Words and Music by
EDDIE ESPINOSA

Melody:

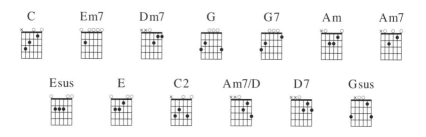

Chorus

C   Em7   Dm7 G   G7 C
Change my heart, O God,   Make it ever true.
Am   **Am7 Dm7 G7**   **C**
Change my heart, O God,   May I be like You.

Verse

Esus E   **Am Dm7 G7   C2 C**
You are the Potter;   I am the clay.
Esus E   **Am**   **Am7/D**
Mold me and make me;
      D7 Gsus G
This is what I   pray.

Come, Now Is the Time to Worship

Words and Music by
BRIAN DOERKSEN

Melody:

Come, now is the time

D	Dsus	A	Em7	G	Bm	Asus

Chorus

D   **Dsus** **D**
Come, now is the time to wor-   ship.
A   **Em7** **G**
Come, now is the time to give your heart.
D   **Dsus** **D**
Come, just as you are, to wor-   ship.
A   **Em7** **G** **D**
Come, just as you are, before your God. Come.

Verse

G   **D**
One day every tongue will confess You are God,
G   **D**
One day every knee will bow.
G   **Bm**
Still, the greatest treasure remains for those
Em7   **Asus** **A**
Who gladly choose You now.

Days of Elijah

Words and Music by
ROBIN MARK

Melody:

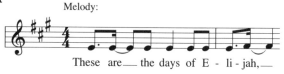

These are⎯ the days of E - li - jah,⎯

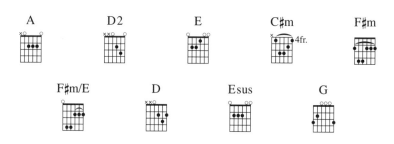

A   D2   E   C♯m   F♯m

F♯m/E   D   Esus   G

Verse 1

    A   D2   A   E   A
These are the days of Elijah, declaring the word of the Lord.
                      D2
And these are the days of Your servant, Moses,
    A   E   A
Righteousness being restored.
       C♯m   F♯m   F♯m/E
And though these are days of great trials
       D   Esus   E
Of famine and darkness and sword,
      A   D2
Still we are the voice in the desert crying,
        A   Esus   E   A
"Prepare ye the way   of the Lord."

Chorus   **Esus E A**   **D**
                Behold,   He comes riding on the clouds,
                            A   **E**
                Shining like the sun, at the trumpet call.
                Esus E A   **D**
                So lift   your voice, it's the year of Jubilee,
                             A   **E**
                And out of Zion's hill salvation comes.

Verse 2   **A**   **D2**
                And these are the days of Ezekiel,
                A   **E**   **A**
                The dry bones becoming as flesh.
                                       D2
                And these are the days of Your servant David,
                A   **E**   **A**
                Rebuilding a temple of praise.
                C♯m   **F♯m**   **F♯m/E**
                And these are the days of the harvest,
                D   **Esus E**
                The fields are as white in the world.
                  A   **D2**
                And we are the laborers in Your vineyard,
                A   **Esus E A**
                Declaring the word of the Lord.

Bridge   **Esus A**   **G**   **D A**
                Who   was, and who is, and who is to come!
                      A   **G**   **D**   **A**
                Who was, and who is, and who is to come, to come, to come!

Cry of My Heart

Words and Music by
TERRY BUTLER

Melody:

It is the cry of my heart to fol - low You.

D   G   A   F♯   A/C♯   Bm   G/B   E7/G♯

Chorus

D   G   A   G
It is the cry of my heart   to follow You.

D   G   A   G
It is the cry of my heart   to be close to You.

D   G   A   F♯
It is the cry of my heart   to follow

G   A   D   (A/C♯)
All of the days of my life.

Verse 1

Bm   G/B   A   D
Teach me Your holy   ways, O Lord,

Bm   E7/G♯   A
So I can walk in Your truth.

Bm   G/B   A   D
Teach me Your holy   ways, O Lord,

G   A   D G   A
And make me wholly devoted to You.

Verse 2

Bm   G/B   A   D
Open my eyes so I can see

Bm   E7/G♯   A
The wonderful things that You do.

Bm   G/B   A   D
Open my heart up more and more,

G   A   D G   A
And make me wholly devoted to You.

Draw Me Close

Words and Music by
KELLY CARPENTER

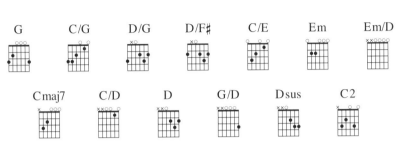

Draw me close — to You,

| G | C/G | D/G | D/F♯ | C/E | Em | Em/D |
| Cmaj7 | C/D | D | G/D | Dsus | C2 | |

Verse

G   **C/G   D/G**   **G**
Draw me close to You,   never let me go,

D/F♯   **C/E**   **Em**
   I lay it all down again,

Em/D   **Cmaj7**   **C/D   D**
To hear You say that I'm Your friend.

G   **C/G   D/G**   **G**
You are my desire,   no one else will do,

D/F♯   **C/E**
   'Cause nothing else could take Your place,

Em   Em/D   **Cmaj7**   **C/D   D**
   To feel the warmth of Your embrace.

G/D   **C/D   Dsus**   **D**   **G   C/D   D**
   Help me find the way,   bring me back to You.

Chorus

G   **D/G   C/G   G**   **D/F♯   C/E   Dsus**
   You're all   I   want,   You're all I've ever   needed.

G   **D/G   C/G   C2**   **D**   **G**
   You're all   I   want,   help me know You are near.

Enough

Words and Music by
CHRIS TOMLIN
and LOUIE GIGLIO

Melody:

All of You— is more than e-nough

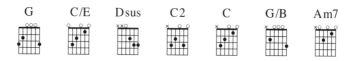

Chorus

G   C/E   Dsus   C2   G
All of You is more than enough for   all of me,
C/E   Dsus   C2   G
For every thirst and   every need.
C/E   Dsus   C   G/B
You satisfy   me   with Your love,
C2   Dsus   G
And all I have in You is more than enough.
C/E   Dsus   C2   G   C/E   Dsus   C2

Verse 1

G   C2   Dsus   G/B   C2
You're my supply, my breath of life;
Am7   Dsus
Still more awesome than I know.
G   C2   Dsus   G/B   C2
You're my reward, worth living for;
Am7   Dsus
Still more awesome than I know.

Verse 2   **G**   **C2 Dsus G/B C2**

            You're my sacri-fice of greatest price;

            Am7   **Dsus**

            Still more awesome than I know.

            G   **C2   Dsus**   **G/B C2**

            You're my coming King, You are every- thing;

            Am7   **Dsus**

            Still more awesome than I know.

Bridge   **G**   **C2 Dsus**   **C2 G/B**

            More than all I want, more than all I need,

            C2   **Dsus**

            You are more than enough for me.

            G   **C2 Dsus**   **C2**   **G/B**

            More than all I know, more than all I can see.

            C2   **Dsus**

            You are more than enough.

Everyday

Words and Music by
JOEL HOUSTON

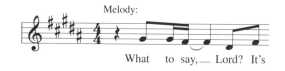

Melody:

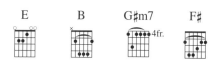

What to say, — Lord? It's

E B G#m7 F#

Verse 1

E   B   G#m7   F#
What to say, Lord? It's You who gave me life,
  E   B   G#m7   F#
And I can't explain just how much You mean to me
E   B   G#m7
Now that You have saved me, Lord.
   F#   E
I give all that I am to You,
   B G#m7 F#   E
That every day I can be a light that shines Your name.
B G#m7 F# E B G#m7 F#

Verse 2

E   B   G#m7   F#   E
Every day, Lord, I'll learn to stand upon Your Word.
   B   G#m7   F#   E
And I pray that I, that I may come to know You more,
     B   G#m7   F#
That You would guide me in every single step I take,
   E   B G#m7   F#   B
That every day I can be Your light unto the world.

© Copyright 1999 Joel Houston / Hillsong Publishing (ASCAP)
(Administered in the US and Canada by Integrity's Hosanna! Music)
(c/o Integrity Media, Inc., 1000 Cody Road, Mobile, AL 36695).

Chorus   (B)   E   G♯m7 F♯
               Every day, it's You I'll live for.
           B   E   G♯m7 F♯   B
           Every day, I'll follow after You.
               E   G♯m7   F♯   B E G♯m7 F♯
           Every day, I'll walk with You, my Lord.
           (repeat)

Bridge   B   E   G♯m7 F♯
           It's You I live for every day.
              B   E   G♯m7 F♯
           It's You I live for every day.
              B   E   G♯m7 F♯ B E G♯m7 F♯
           It's You I live for every day.

Everyone Arise

Words and Music by
TOMMY WALKER

Melody:

Ev-'ry - one a - rise and— let it shine.—

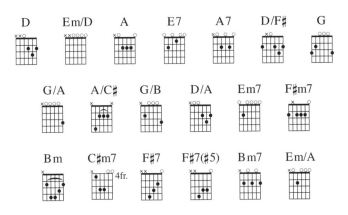

Verse

                 D   **Em/D** **D**
Everyone arise and let   it   shine.
               A   **E7**   **A7**
Children of our God, your light has come,
        D/F♯   **G**
For the glory of the Lord,
                    D/F♯   **E7**   **A** **E7** **A**
And the beauty of His grace is rising on you now.
G/A   **D**   **A/C♯** **G/B**
Though the darkness covers all the earth,
D/A   **A**   **E7**   **A7**
They will see your light, they will hear the sound,
        D/F♯   **G**   **D**
For the glory of the Lord, and the beauty of His grace
               Em/D **D** **G/A**
Is rising on you now.

Chorus

D   **A/C♯**   **G/B** **D/A**
Praise Him, praise Him, praise Him.
 G   **D/F♯**   **Em7** **F♯m7** **G**   **A**
Arise and shine and cel-   e-   brate Him.
D   **A/C♯**   **G/B** **D/A**
Praise Him, praise Him, praise Him.
G   **D/F♯** **Em7** **G/A**
Let His glory   rise   on   you,
             G **D/F♯** **Bm** **A** **(D)**
Let it rise.

Bridge

              C♯m7 **F♯7** **C♯m7**
There's just some- thing
   F♯7   **Bm**   **F♯7(♯5)** **Bm7**
So right about lifting His name on high.
          C♯m7 **F♯7** **C♯m7** **F♯7**
It brings us joy   and peace of mind
        G   **Em/A** **D/A** **G/A**
When we give our lives to glo-   ri-   fy Him.

Every Move I Make

Words and Music by
DAVID RUIS

Melody:

La la la la la la la,   La la la la la la la!

G   C   D   Dsus   Am7   Bm7   D7sus

Intro   G   C   D   C   (G)
La la la la la la la, La la la la la la la!

Verse   G   C   Dsus
Every move I make, I make in You,
                  C
You make me move, Jesus.
G   C   Dsus C
Every breath I take, I breathe in You.
G   C   Dsus   C
Every step I take, I take in You, You are my way, Jesus.
G   C   Dsus C
Every breath I take, I breathe in You.

Chorus   G   Am7 Bm7   C D7sus
Waves of mercy, waves of grace,
G   Am7   Bm7 C D7sus G
Everywhere I look,   I see Your   face.
    Am7   Bm7   C D7sus
Your love has captured me.
G   Am7   Bm7
O, my God, this love,
    C D7sus G C D C G C D C
How can it   be?

Famous One

Words and Music by
CHRIS TOMLIN
and JESSE REEVES

Melody:

You___ are the Lord, ___

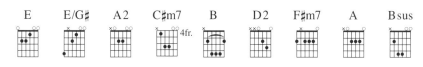

E   E/G♯   A2   C♯m7   B   D2   F♯m7   A   Bsus

Section

    E   **E/G♯**   **A2**
You are the Lord, the famous One, famous One;
C♯m7   **B**   **A2**
Great is Your name in all   the earth.
        E   **E/G♯**   **A2**
The heavens declare You're glorious, glorious;

Section

C♯m7   **B**   **E**   **(D2   A2)**
Great is Your fame beyond   the earth.

           F♯m7   **C♯m7**
And for all You've done and yet to do,
       A   **E**
With every breath I'm praising You.

Section

    F♯m7   **C♯m7**
Desire of nations and every heart,
     A2   **Bsus**
You alone are God, You alone are God.

      F♯m7   **C♯m7**
The Morning Star is shining through,
      A   **E**
And every eye is watching You.
    F♯m7   **C♯m7**
Reveal Thy nature and miracles.
    A2   **Bsus**
You are beautiful, You are beautiful.

Forever

Words and Music by
CHRIS TOMLIN

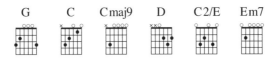

Give thanks to the Lord— our God and— King;—

G   C   Cmaj9   D   C2/E   Em7

Verse 1

G
Give thanks to the Lord our God and King;

His love endures forever.
C
For He is good, He is above all things;
Cmaj9   **G**
His love endures forever.

Pre-Chorus

D   **C2/E**
Sing praise, sing praise.

Verse 2

G
With a mighty hand and outstretched arm;

His love endures forever.
C
For the life that's been reborn;
Cmaj9   **G**
His love endures forever.

Chorus   **G**   **Em7**

Forever God is faithful, forever God is strong,

              D   **C**

Forever God is with us, forever.

              G   **Em7**

Forever God is faithful, forever God is strong,

              D   **C**   **G**

Forever God is with us, forever. Forever.

Verse 3   **G**

From the rising to the setting sun

His love endures forever.

                   C

And by the grace of God we will carry on;

        Cmaj9   **G**

His love endures forever.

Friend of God

Words and Music by
MICHAEL GUNGOR and
ISRAEL HOUGHTON

Melody:

Who am I___ that You___ are

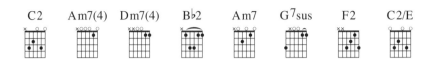

C2   Am7(4)   Dm7(4)   B♭2   Am7   G⁷sus   F2   C2/E

Verse

C2   **Am7(4)**
Who am I that You are mindful of me?
     Dm7(4)   **C2**
That You hear me when I call?
                         Am7(4)
Is it true that You are thinking of me?
     Dm7(4)   **B♭2**
How You love me, it's amazing.

Chorus

C2   **Am7**
I am a friend of God. I am a friend of God.
Dm7(4)   **G7sus**   **C2**
I am a friend of God, He calls me friend.
C2   **Am7**
I am a friend of God. I am a friend of God.
Dm7(4)   **G7sus**   **C2**
I am a friend of God, He calls me friend.

Bridge

F2   **C2/E**   **Dm7(4)**   **F2**
God Almighty, Lord of Glory, You have called me friend.
F2   **C2/E**   **Dm7(4)**   **F2**
God Almighty, Lord of Glory, You have called me friend.

Give Thanks

Words and Music by
HENRY SMITH

Give thanks with a grate-ful heart.

F   C/E   Dm   Am   B♭   F/A   E♭   C7sus

C7   Am7   Dm7   C/D   Gm7   B♭/C   B♭/F

Verse
        F   **C/E**
Give thanks with a grateful heart.
        Dm   **Am**
Give thanks to the Holy One.
        B♭   **F/A**
Give thanks because He's given
F   **E♭**   **C7sus**   **C7**
Jesus Christ, His Son.

Chorus
        Am7   **Dm7**   **C/D** **Dm7** **Gm7**
And now let the weak say, "I   am   strong,"
        C7   **B♭/C** **C7** **F**
Let the poor say, "I   am rich
        Dm7   **E♭**   **C7sus** **C7**
Because of what the Lord has done for us."

Tag
        F   **B♭/F**   **F**   **B♭/F**   **F**
Give thanks,   give thanks,   give thanks.

God of Wonders

Words and Music by
MARK BYRD and
STEVE HINDALONG

Lord of all___ cre - a - tion,___

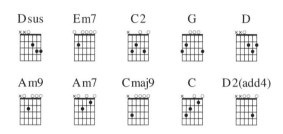

Verse 1

Dsus   Em7   C2   Dsus   Em7   C2
Lord of all creation,   of water, earth and sky,

Dsus   Em7   C2
The heavens are Your tabernacle;

Dsus   Em7   C2
Glory to the Lord on high.

Chorus

G   Dsus   D
God of wonders beyond our galaxy,

        Am9   Am7   Cmaj9   C
You are ho-   ly,   ho-   ly;

G   Dsus   D
The universe declares Your majesty,

        Am9   Am7   Cmaj9   C
You are ho-   ly,   ho-   ly;

C   D2(add4)   C   D2(add4)   C
Lord of heaven and earth, Lord of heaven and earth.

Verse 2   **Dsus** **Em7**   **C2**
                   Early in the morning
          Dsus   **Em7**   **C2**
                   I will celebrate the light.
          Dsus   **Em7**   **C2**
                   When I stumble in the darkness
          Dsus   **Em7**   **C2**
                   I will call Your name by night.

Bridge   **Am7**   **C2**   **Dsus**
                   Hallelujah to the Lord of heaven and earth,
          Am7   **C2**   **Dsus**
                   Hallelujah to the Lord of heaven and earth,
          Am7   **C2**   **Dsus**   **G**
                   Hallelujah to the Lord of heaven and earth!

Great Is the Lord

Words and Music by
MICHAEL W. SMITH
and DEBORAH D. SMITH

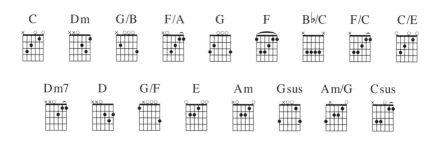

Verse
C   Dm   G/B C
Great is the Lord, He is holy and just;
   F/A G   F C
By His power we trust in His love.
C   Dm   G/B   C
Great is the Lord, He is faithful and true;
   F/A G   F C
By His mercy He proves He is love.

Chorus 1   **B♭/C   F/C   B♭/C   F   C/E   Dm7   C**
Great is the   Lord and worthy   of   glory!
B♭/C   F/C   B♭/C   F/C   G   C
Great is the   Lord   and   worthy of praise.
B♭/C   F/C   B♭/C   D   G
Great is the   Lord; now lift up your voice,
G/F   E   Am
Now   lift up your voice:
Dm   Gsus   G   Am   Am/G
Great   is the Lord!
Dm   Gsus   G   C (Csus C)
Great   is the Lord!

Chorus 2   **B♭/C   F/C   B♭/C   F   C/E   Dm7   C**
Great are You,   Lord and worthy   of   glory!
B♭/C   F/C   B♭/C   F/C   G   C
Great are You,   Lord   and   worthy of praise.
B♭/C   F/C   B♭/C   D   G
Great are You,   Lord; I lift up my voice,
G/F   E   Am
I   lift up my voice:
Dm   Gsus   G   Am   Am/G
Great   are You, Lord!
Dm   Gsus   G   C   Csus   C
Great   are You, Lord!

Grace Flows Down

Words and Music by
DAVID BELL, LOUIE GIGLIO
and ROD PADGETT

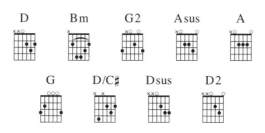

Verse

D   Bm G2   Asus   A
Amazing grace,   how sweet the sound;

D   Bm G2   Asus   A
Amazing love,   now flowing down

G   Asus   A
From hands and feet

            D   D/C♯ Bm   A
That were nailed to the tree

G   Asus   A   D Dsus D
As grace flows down and covers me.

Chorus

            G2 Asus A   G2 Asus A
It covers me,   it covers me,

            G2 Asus A
It covers me,

            D2 Bm G2 Asus   A   D
And covers me.

Hallelujah
(Your Love Is Amazing)

Words and Music by
BRENTON BROWN and
BRIAN DOERKSEN

Melody:

Your love is a - maz - ing,

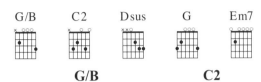

G/B   C2   Dsus   G   Em7

Verse 1

                G/B   **C2**
Your love is amazing, steady and unchanging.
               Dsus   **C2**
Your love is a mountain firm beneath my feet.
                G/B   **C2**
Your love is a mystery, how You gently lift me.
               Dsus   **C2**
When I am surrounded Your love carries me.

Chorus

        G   **Dsus**   **Em7** **C2**
Hallelujah, hallelujah, hallelujah, Your love makes me sing.
        G   **Dsus**   **Em7** **C2**
Hallelujah, hallelujah, hallelujah, Your love makes me sing.

Verse 2

                G/B   **C2**
Your love is surprising. I can feel it rising,
               Dsus   **C2**
All the joy that's growing deep inside of me.
                G/B   **C2**
Every time I see You all Your goodness shines through.
               Dsus   **C2**
I can feel this God song rising up in me.

Tag

        C2   **G**
Lord, You make me sing. How You make me sing.

He Has Made Me Glad

(I Will Enter His Gates)

Words and Music by
LEONA VON BRETHORST

Melody:

I will en-ter His gates

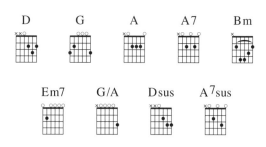

Verse

            D   **G**   **D**
I will enter His gates with thanksgiving in my heart;
            D   **G**   **A A7**
I will enter His courts with praise.
            D   **G**   **D**   **Bm**
I will say, "This is the day that the Lord has made!"
Em7   **A7**   **D G/A**
I will rejoice for He has made me glad.

Chorus   **D**   **G**   **D**   **Bm**
He has made me glad, He has made me glad,
      Em7   **A7**   **D Dsus A7sus A7**
I will rejoice for He has made me glad.
      D   **G**   **D**   **Bm**
He has made me glad, He has made me glad,
      Em7   **A7**   **D**
I will rejoice for He has made me glad.

He Is Exalted

Words and Music by
TWILA PARIS

Melody:

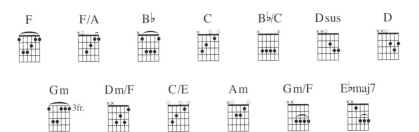

He is ex-alt-ed, the King is ex-alt-ed on___ high,

| F | F/A | B♭ | C | B♭/C | Dsus | D |
| Gm | Dm/F | C/E | Am | Gm/F | E♭maj7 |

Verse

    F   **F/A**   **B♭**
He is exalted, the King is exalted on high,
                     C
I will praise Him.
    F   **F/A**
He is exalted, forever exalted
          B♭ **C** **B♭/C** **C** **Dsus** **D**
And I   will praise His name!

Chorus

    Gm **Dm/F** **C/E** **C**   **F**   **Am**   **B♭** **F/A**
He   is the Lord,   forever His truth shall reign.
    Gm **Dm/F** **C/E** **C**   **F**   **Am** **B♭** **F/A**
Heav-en and earth   rejoice in His holy name.
    Gm   **Gm/F**   **E♭maj7** **B♭/C**   **F**
He is exalted, the King is exalted on high!

Hear Our Praises

Words and Music by
REUBEN MORGAN

Melody:

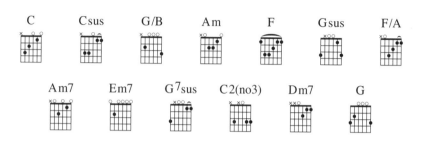

May our homes ___ be filled ___

C Csus G/B Am F Gsus F/A

Am7 Em7 G7sus C2(no3) Dm7 G

Verse 1

C   **Csus**   C   G/B

May our homes be filled with dancing,

Am   **F**   **Gsus**

May our streets be filled with joy;

C   **Csus**   C   G/B   **Am**

May injustice bow to Jesus

F   **Gsus**

As the people turn to pray.

Chorus

C   G/B   F/A

From the mountain   to the valley

Am7 Em7   F   **Gsus**

Hear our praises   rise to You;

G7sus C   G/B   F/A

From the heavens   to the nations,

Am7 Em7

Hear our singing

F Gsus C **Csus** C **Csus**

Fill the air.

Verse 2   **C**   **Csus**   **C**   **G/B**
          May a light shine in the darkness
        Am   **F**   **Gsus**
          As we walk before the cross;
        C   **Csus**   **C**   **G/B** **Am**
          May Your glory fill the whole earth
        F   **Gsus**
     As the water o'er the seas.

Bridge   **C2(no3)** **C**   **F**   **Dm7**   **Am7** **Em7**
            Hallelujah,   Hallelujah,
        F   **Dm7**   **Gsus** **G**
   Hallelujah,   Hallelujah!

Here I Am to Worship

Words and Music by
TIM HUGHES

Melody:

Light of the World, You stepped down

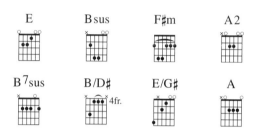

E	B sus	F♯m	A 2

B⁷sus	B/D♯	E/G♯	A

Verse 1

    E   **Bsus**   **F♯m**
Light of the World, You stepped down into darkness,
    E   **Bsus**   **A2**
Opened my eyes, let me see.
    E   **Bsus**   **F♯m**
Beauty that made this heart adore You,
    E   **Bsus**   **A2**
Hope of a life spent with You.

Chorus

         B7sus **E**   **B/D♯**
So, here I am to worship, here I am to bow down,
           E/G♯   **A2**
Here I am to say that You're my God.
                      E   **B/D♯**
You're altogether lovely, altogether worthy,
       E/G♯   **A2** **B7sus** **(E)**
Altogether wonderful to me.

Verse 2   **E**   **Bsus**   **F♯m**
King of all days, oh so highly exalted,
E   **Bsus**   **A2**
Glorious in heaven above.
E   **Bsus**   **F♯m**
Humbly You came to the earth You created,
E   **Bsus**   **A2**
All for love's sake became poor.

Bridge   **B/D♯** **E/G♯**   **A**
And I'll never   know how much it cost
B/D♯ **E/G♯** **A**
To see my sin   upon that cross.

He Knows My Name

Words and Music by
TOMMY WALKER

Melody:

I have— a Mak - er,—

E   F♯m7   E/G♯   A   E/B

B   B7sus   Esus/F♯   C♯m7

Verse 1

E   F♯m7   E/G♯   A   E/B   B   B7sus
I have a Mak- er,   He formed my heart.
E   F♯m7   E/G♯   A
Before even time began
E/B   B   B7sus   E   Esus/F♯   E/G♯
My life was in   His   hands.

Chorus

A   E   B   E   A   E   B   E
He knows my name.   He knows my every thought.
A   E   B   C♯m7   F♯m7   B   E
He sees each tear that falls, and hears me when I call.
(**B7sus** - *1st time*)   (**Esus/F♯**   **E/G♯** - *2nd time*)

Verse 2

E   F♯m7   E/G♯   A   E/B   B   B7sus
I have a Fa-   ther,   He calls me His own.
E   F♯m7   E/G♯   A
He'll never   leave   me
E/B   B   B7sus   E   Esus/F♯   E/G♯
No matter where I   go.

Tag

A   B   C♯m7   F♯m7   B   E
He hears me when I call, And He hears me when I call.

Holy and Anointed One

Words and Music by
JOHN BARNETT

Melody:

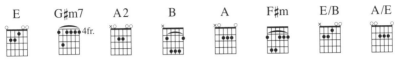

Je - sus,

E G#m7 A2 B A F#m E/B A/E

F#m/E A/C# F#m/A C#m F#m/B A2/C# E/G#

Verse

E G#m7 A2 E B A2
Je-   sus, Je-   sus,

E   B   A   F#m   E/B B E
Holy and Anointed One, Je-   sus.

E G#m7 A2 E B A2
Je-   sus, Je-   sus,

E   B   A   F#m   E/B B   E
Risen and Exalted One, Je-   sus.

Chorus

A/E E F#m/E A/E A   E
Your name is like   hon- ey on my lips.

A/E E F#m/E A/E A   E
Your Spir- it is   wa- ter to my soul.

E/B A/C# E/B F#m/A A/C#   G#m7 C#m
Your Word is   a   lamp unto my   feet.

A   F#m/B
Jesus, I love You. I love You.

Tag

E G#m7 A2
Je-   sus,

E B A2/C# E/G# A E/G# F#m E
Je- sus.

Holy Is the Lord

Words and Music by
JEFF SEARLES

Melody:

Ho - ly is— the— Lord.—

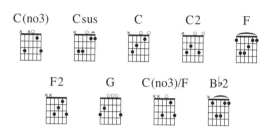

C(no3) Csus C C2 F

F2 G C(no3)/F B♭2

Verse 1

C(no3) Csus C   Csus C C2
Ho-   ly   is the Lord.
C(no3) Csus C   Csus C C2
Ho-   ly   is the Lord.
     F F2 F   C Csus C
As we bow   before Your throne,
C2 G   F   C Csus C
Majesty and honor to You alone.
C2 G   F   C Csus C C2
Majesty and honor to You alone.

Verse 2

C(no3) Csus C   Csus C C2
Wor-   thy are You, Lord.
C(no3) Csus C   Csus C C2
Wor-   thy are You, Lord.
     F F2 F   C Csus C
Sweet Lamb of God, the chosen One.
   C2   G   F   C Csus C
Our lives we gladly lay before Your throne.
   C2   G   F   C Csus C C2
Our lives we gladly lay before Your throne.

Pre- **G**   **F**
Chorus   No longer will we give our hearts
                C   **G**
        To the things of this world.
                          F   **C**
        For a debt of love we will offer to You.
        G   **F**   **C**
            We look for the day when every knee will bow.
        G   **F**   **C**
            We will join with the angels around Your throne,
                        G   **F**
        And we will sing.

Chorus   **C(no3)**   **C(no3)/F**
                    Holy is the Lord.   *(sing three times)*
            B♭2   **F**   **C**
                Ho-   ly is the Lord.

How Deep the Father's Love for Us

Words and Music by
STUART TOWNEND

Melody:

How deep the Fa-ther's love for us,

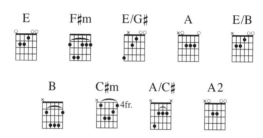

Verse 1

            E   F♯m   E/G♯   A
How deep the Father's love   for   us,

E/G♯   E/B   B
How vast beyond all meas-   ure

            E   F♯m   E/G♯   A
That He should give His on-   ly   Son

E/G♯   B   E
To make a wretch His treasure.

                   F♯m   E/G♯   A
How great the pain of sear-   ing   loss.

E/G♯   C♯m   B
The Father turns His face   away

           E   F♯m   E/G♯   A
As wounds which mar the Cho-   sen   One

E/G♯   B   E   A/C♯   E/B   E   A2
Bring many sons to glo-ry.

Verse 2

E   F♯m E/G♯ A
Behold the Man upon a cross,
 E/G♯   E/B B
My sin upon His shoul- ders.
 E   F♯m E/G♯ A
Ashamed, I hear my mock- ing voice
 E/G♯   B E
Call out among the scoffers.
       F♯m E/G♯ A
It was my sin that held Him there
 E/G♯   C♯m B
Until it was accom- plished;
 E   F♯m E/G♯ A
His dying breath has brought me life.
 E/G♯   B E A/C♯ E/B E A2
I know that it is fin- ished.

Verse 3

 E   F♯m E/G♯ A
I will not boast in an- y- thing:
 E/G♯   E/B B
No gifts, no pow'r, no wis- dom.
 E   F♯m E/G♯ A
But I will boast in Je- sus Christ:
 E/G♯   B E
His death and resurrec- tion.
       F♯m E/G♯ A
Why should I gain from His re- ward?
 E/G♯   C♯m B
I cannot give an an- swer.
  E   F♯m E/G♯ A
But this I know with all my heart:
 E/G♯   B E
His wounds have paid my ran- som.

How Great Thou Art

Words and Music by
STUART K. HINE

Melody:

O Lord, my God, when I in awe-some won-der

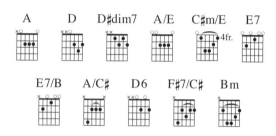

Verse 1

        A   **D**

O Lord, my God, when I in awesome wonder

    D♯dim7 **A/E** **C♯m/E**   **E7**   **A**

Consider   all the worlds Thy hands have made,

              D

I see the stars, I hear the rolling thunder,

    D♯dim7 **A/E** **C♯m/E** **E7**   **A**

Thy pow'r thro'-   out the uni-   verse displayed.

Chorus

                D   **A**

Then sings my soul, my Savior God, to Thee,

      E7   **A**

How great Thou art! How great Thou art!

                D   **A**

Then sings my soul, my Savior God, to Thee;

    E7/B **A/C♯** **D6** **F♯7/C♯** **Bm** **E7** **A**

How great   Thou   art! How   great Thou art!

Verse 2

               A   **D**
When thro' the woods and forest glades I wander
         D♯dim7 **A/E**   **C♯m/E** **E7** **A**
And hear the   birds sing sweetly in the trees,
                         D
When I look down from lofty mountain grandeur,
         D♯dim7 **A/E**   **C♯m/E** **E7** **A**
And hear the   brook and feel the gentle breeze;

Verse 3

               A   **D**
And when I think that God, His Son not sparing,
         D♯dim7 **A/E** **C♯m/E**   **E7**   **A**
Sent Him to   die, I scarce can take it in;
                        D
That on the cross, my burden gladly bearing,
         D♯dim7 **A/E** **C♯m/E** **E7**   **A**
He bled and   died to take   away my sin.

Verse 4

               A   **D**
When Christ shall come with shout of acclamation
         D♯dim7 **A/E**   **C♯m/E** **E7**   **A**
And take me   home, what joy shall fill my heart!
                       D
Then I shall bow in humble adoration
         D♯dim7 **A/E**   **C♯m/E** **E7**   **A**
And there pro-   claim: my God, how great Thou art!

How Great Is Our God

Words and Music by
CHRIS TOMLIN, ED CASH
and JESSE REEVES

Melody:

The splen-dor of___ the King___

C2   Am7   F2   G

Verse 1

       C2   **Am7**
The splendor of the King clothed in majesty,
          F2
Let all the earth rejoice, let all the earth rejoice.
    C2   **Am7**
He wraps Himself in light and darkness tries to hide.
         F2
It trembles at His voice, it trembles at His voice.

Chorus

       C2
How great is our God!
         Am7
Sing with me. How great is our God!
               F2   **G**   **C2**
And all will see how great, how great is our God.

Verse 2   **C2**   **Am7**
Age to age, He stands and time is in His hands,
         F2
Beginning and the End, Beginning and the End.
    C2   **Am7**
The Godhead, three in one, Father, Spirit, Son,
         F2
The Lion and the Lamb, the Lion and the Lamb.

Bridge   **C2**   **Am7**
Name above all names, worthy of all praise,
    F2   **G**   **C2**
My heart will sing. How great is our God!

Hunger and Thirst

Words and Music by
DAVID MOFFITT and SUE C. SMITH

Melody:

I hun - ger— and thirst— for You.—

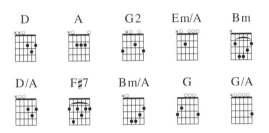

Chorus   D   A   G2   Em/A
I hunger and thirst for You.
     D   A   Bm   G2
I hunger and thirst for You.
Em/A   D   G2   D/A   G2
In the desert of my need, You're the fountain that I seek.
        D/A   F♯7   Bm   Bm/A
You're the Living Water I keep running to.
  G2   A   Bm   D/A
I hunger and thirst for You.
  G   G/A   D
I hunger and thirst for You.

Hungry
(Falling on My Knees)

Words and Music by
KATHRYN SCOTT

Melody:

Hun - gry,   I___ come   to___ You,

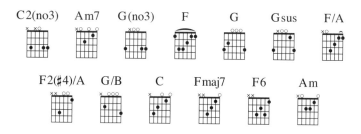

C2(no3)	Am7	G(no3)	F	G	Gsus	F/A

F2(♯4)/A	G/B	C	Fmaj7	F6	Am

Verse 1

C2(no3)   Am7   G(no3)   F
Hungry, I come to You, for I know You satisfy.
C2(no3)   Am7   G(no3)   F
I am empty, but I know Your love does not run dry.

*Pre-
Chorus*

G Gsus   F/A F2(♯4)/A F/A G/B F
So I wait   for You.   So I wait for You.

Chorus

C   Fmaj7 F6 C   Fmaj7 F6
I'm falling on my knees,   offering all of me.
C   Fmaj7 F6 C Am G(no3) F
Jesus, You're all this heart is living for.

Verse 2

C2(no3)   Am7   G(no3)   F
Broken, I run to You, for Your arms are open wide;
C2(no3)   Am7   G(no3)   F
I am weary, but I know Your touch restores my life.

I Could Sing of Your Love Forever

Words and Music by
MARTIN SMITH

Melody:

O - ver the moun - tains and the sea

E   F#m7(add4)   A2   Bsus   E/G#

Verse   **E**   **F#m7(add4)**
          Over the mountains and the sea

          Your river runs with love for me,
          A2   **Bsus**
          And I will open up my heart and let the Healer set me free.
          E   **F#m7(add4)**
          I'm happy to be in the truth, and I will daily lift my hands
          A2   **Bsus**
          For I will always sing of when Your love came down. Yeah!

Chorus **E**   **F#m7(add4)**
          I could sing of Your love forever,

          A2   **Bsus**
          I could sing of Your love forever.

Bridge **F#m7(add4)**   **E/G#**
          O I feel like dancing.

          A2   **Bsus**
          It's foolishness, I know.

          F#m7(add4)   **E/G#**
          But when the world has seen the light

                A2   **Bsus**
          They will dance with joy like we're dancing now.

I Give You My Heart

Words and Music by
REUBEN MORGAN

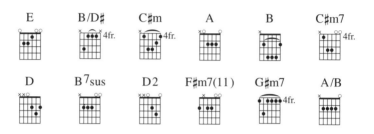

Verse

E   B/D♯ C♯m A   E   B
This is my de-   sire, to hon-or   You.
C♯m7   B/D♯ E   D   A   B7sus
Lord, with all my   heart I worship You.
        E   B/D♯ C♯m A   E   B
With all I have with-   in me, I give You praise.
C♯m7   B/D♯ E   D2   D   A   B7sus
All that I a-   dore is in You.

Chorus

E   B   F♯m7(11)
    Lord, I give You my heart, I give You my soul.
B7sus   E
I live for You alone.
            B/D♯   F♯m7(11)
Every breath that I take, every moment I'm awake,
    B7sus   E   (G♯m7   A/B)
Lord, have Your way in me.

I Love You, Lord

Words and Music by
LAURIE KLEIN

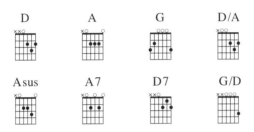

Chorus

    D   **A** **D**
I love You, Lord, and I lift my voice
   G **D/A** **A** **D/A** **A** **Asus** **A7**
To worship   You, O my soul re-   joice!
   D   **A** **D**
Take joy, my King, in what You hear:
D7   **G**   **D/A** **A**   **A7** **D** **G/D** **D**
May it be a sweet, sweet sound in Your ear.

I Stand in Awe

Words and Music by
MARK ALTROGGE

Melody:

You are beau-ti-ful___ be-yond de-scrip-tion,___

D13   G2   Gmaj7   C/G   G   C   D/C

D   Am/C   B7   Em   A7sus   A7   D7sus

D7   C/D   D/G   B7sus   Cmaj7   G/B   Am7

Verse

      D13   G2   Gmaj7
You are beautiful beyond description,
      C/G   G2
Too marvelous for words;
           C/G G   C/G G
Too wonderful for com-   prehen-   sion,
      C   D/C C D Am/C B7
Like nothing ever seen   or   heard.
      Em   A7sus   A7
Who can grasp Your infinite wisdom?
      C   D
Who can fathom the depth of Your love?
      G2   Gmaj7
You are beautiful beyond description,
      C D7sus D7 G C/D
Majesty enthroned a-   bove.

Chorus

           G   **D/G**   **D/C** **C**   **C/D**
And I stand, I stand in awe   of You,

 G   **D/G**   **D/C** **C**
I stand, I stand in awe   of You;

    B7sus **B7**   **Cmaj7** **Am/C** **C** **G/B**
Holy God, to whom all praise   is   due,

   Am7   **D7**   **C/G** **G**
I stand in awe of You.

I Want to Know You

(In the Secret)

Words and Music by
ANDY PARK

Melody:

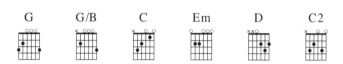

In the se - cret, in the qui - et place,——

G	G/B	C	Em	D	C2

Verse 1

G   G/B   C
In the secret,   in the quiet place,
Em   D   C2
In the stillness, You are there.
G   G/B   C
In the secret,   in the quiet hour I wait only for You,
Em   D   C2
'Cause I want to know You more.

Chorus

G   D   Em   C2
I want to know You,   I want to hear Your voice,
G   D   C G/B C
I want to know You more.
G   D   Em   C2
I want to touch You,   I want to see Your face,
G   D   C G/B C
I want to know You more.

Verse 2

```
          G              G/B              C
     I am reaching    for the highest goal,
     Em               D       C2
          That I might receive the prize.
     G                 G/B
        Pressing onward,
                       C
     Pushing every hindrance aside, out of my way,
     Em               D       C2
          'Cause I want to know You more.
```

I Will Call Upon the Lord

Words and Music by
MICHAEL O'SHIELDS

Melody:

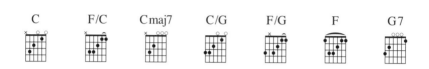

I will call up - on___ the Lord

C   F/C   Cmaj7   C/G   F/G   F   G7

Verse

| C | F/C | | Cmaj7 | F/C |

I will call upon the Lord (I will call upon the Lord)

C   F/C   Cmaj7   F/C

Who is worthy to be praised. (Who is worthy to be praised.)

C   F/C   Cmaj7   F/C

So shall I be saved from my enemies.

            C   F/C

(So shall I be saved from my enemies.)

C/G   F/G   C   F/G

I will call upon the Lord.

Chorus

     C   F   C

The Lord liveth, and blessed be the Rock,

        F   C   G7

And let the God of my salvation be exalted.

     C   F   C

The Lord liveth, and blessed be the Rock,

       F   C   G7   C

And let the God of my salvation be exalt- ed.

I Worship You, Almighty God

Words and Music by
SONDRA CORBETT-WOOD

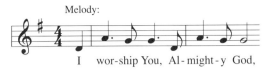

Melody:

I wor-ship You, Al-might-y God,

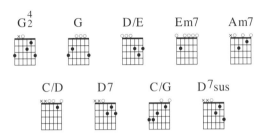

Chorus

G^4_2 G   D/E Em7 Am7
I wor-   ship You, Almight- y God,

           C/D   G C/D
There is none like You.

D7 G4(2) G   D/E Em7   Am7
I   wor-   ship You, O Prince of Peace,

           C/D   D7
That is what I want to do.

C/G G   Em7
I give   You praise

               Am7   D7sus D7
For You are my righteousness.

G4(2) G   D/E Em7 Am7
I wor-   ship You, Almight- y God,

         C/D D7 G
There is none like   You.

In Christ Alone

Words by STUART TOWNEND
Music by KEITH GETTY

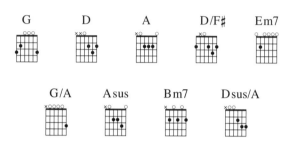

Verse 1

      G   **D**   **G**   **A**
In Christ alone my hope is found,
D/F♯   **G** **D/F♯** **Em7** **G/A**   **D**
He is my light, my   strength,   my song;
      G   **D**   **G**   **A**
This Corner-stone, this solid Ground,
D/F♯   **G** **D/F♯** **Em7** **G/A**   **D**
Firm through the fierc-est   drought   and storm.
      D/F♯ **G**   **D/F♯** **Asus** **A**
What heights of love, what depths of peace,
      D/F♯ **G**   **Bm7** **Asus** **A**
When fears are stilled, when strivings cease!
    G   **D**   **G**   **A**
My Comfort-er, my All in All,
D/F♯   **G** **D/F♯** **Em7** **G/A** **D** **Dsus/A** **D**
Here in the love of   Christ   I stand.

Verse 2

| G | D | G | A |

In Christ alone!– who took on flesh,

| D/F♯ | G | D/F♯ | Em7 | G/A | D |

Fulness of God in   help-   less Babe!

| G | D | G | A |

This gift of love and righteous-ness,

| D/F♯ | G | D/F♯ | Em7 | G/A | D |

Scorned by the ones He   came   to save;

| D/F♯ | G | D/F♯ | Asus | A |

Till on that cross as Jesus   died,

| D/F♯ | G | Bm7 | Asus | A |

The wrath of God was satis- fied–

| G | D | G | A |

For every sin on Him was laid;

| D/F♯ | G | D/F♯ | Em7 | G/A | D | Dsus/A | D |

Here in the death of   Christ   I live.

Additional Verses:

Verse 3   There in the ground His body lay,
Light of the world by darkness slain:
Then bursting forth in glorious Day
Up from the grave He rose again!
And as He stands in victory
Sin's curse has lost its grip on me,
For I am His and He is mine–
Bought with the precious blood of Christ.

Verse 4   No guilt in life, no fear in death,
This is the pow'r of Christ in me;
From life's first cry to final breath,
Jesus commands my destiny.
No pow'r of hell, no scheme of man,
Can ever pluck me from His hand;
Till He returns or calls me home,
Here in the pow'r of Christ I'll stand.

Indescribable

Words and Music by
LAURA STORY

Melody:

From the high - est of heights

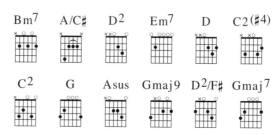

Verse 1   **Bm7**   **A/C#**   **D2**
            From the highest of heights to the depths of the sea,
         Em7   **D   C2(#4)**
            Creation's revealing Your majesty.
         Bm7   **A/C#**   **D2**
            From the colors of fall to the fragrance of spring,
         Em7   **D**   **C2**
            Every creature's unique in a song that it sings.
         G   Asus
         All exclaiming:

Chorus   **D2**   **Asus**
           Indescribable,   uncontainable,
Gmaj9   **Bm7**
You placed the stars in the sky and you know them by name.
D2/F♯   **Gmaj9**
You are amazing God.
D2   **Asus**
    All powerful,   untamable,
Gmaj9   **Bm7**
Awestruck we fall to our knees and we humbly proclaim
   D2/F♯   **Gmaj9**
That You are amazing God.

Verse 2   **Bm7**   **A/C♯**   **D2**
     Who has told every lightning bolt where it should go,
Em7   **D**   **C2(♯4)**
    Or seen heavenly storehouses laden with snow?
Bm7   **A/C♯**   **D2**
    Who imagined the sun and gives source to its light,
Em7   **D**   **C2**
    Yet conceals it to bring us the coolness of night?
G   **Asus**
None can fathom.

Bridge   **Bm7** **D2/F♯**   **Em7** **Bm7**
     You are amazing God.
D2/F♯   **Gmaj7**
You are amazing God.

Alt. Chorus **D2**   **Asus**
    Incomparable,   unchangeable,
Gmaj9   **Bm7**
You see the depths of my heart and You love me the same.
D2/F♯   **Gmaj9**
You are amazing God.

King of Glory

Words and Music by
MAC POWELL, BRAD AVERY,
TAI ANDERSON and DAVID CARR

Melody:

Who is—— this King of glo - ry——

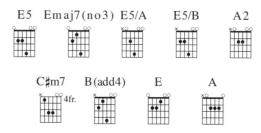

Verse 1

     E5   **Emaj7(no3)**
Who is this King of glory
    E5/A   **E5/B** **E5/A**
That pursues me with His love
    E5   **Emaj7(no3)**
And haunts me with each hearing
    E5/A   **E5/B** **E5/A**
Of His softly spoken words?
    A2   **C♯m7**
My conscience, a reminder of forgiveness that I need;
    B(add4)   **A2**   **E5**
Who is this King of glory   Who offers it to me?

Verse 2   **E5**   **Emaj7(no3)**

Who is this King of angels,

   E5/A   **E5/B**   **E5/A**

O blessed Prince of Peace,

   E5   **Emaj7(no3)**

Revealing things of heaven

   E5/A   **E5/B**   **E5/A**

And all its mysteries?

   A2   **C♯m7**

My spirit's ever longing for His grace in which to stand.

   B(add4)   **A2**

Who is this King of glory,

                  E5   **E**

Son of God, and Son of Man?

Chorus   **A**   **C♯m7**

His name is Jesus, precious Jesus,

   B(add4)   **A2**   **E5**

Lord Almighty, King of my heart, King of glory.

Verse 3   **E5**   **Emaj7(no3)**

Who is this King of glory,

   E5/A   **E5/B**   **E5/A**

With strength and majesty

   E5   **Emaj7(no3)**

And wisdom beyond measure,

   E5/A   **E5/B**   **E5/A**

The gracious King of kings?

   A2   **C♯m7**

The Lord of earth and heaven, the Creator of all things;

   B(add4)   **A2**   **E5**   **E**

He is the King of glory,   He is everything to me.

Knowing You
(All I Once Held Dear)

Words and Music by
GRAHAM KENDRICK

Melody:

All I— once held— dear,

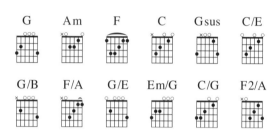

Verse 1

G Am F C   F G C
All I once held dear, built my life up- on,
        Am F C   Am Gsus G
All this world re- veres and wars to own,
C C/E F   G   C   G/B F/A G   C
All I   once thought gain I have count- ed loss,
        G/B Am F C   Am Gsus G
Spent and   worth-less now compared to this.

Chorus   G/E C/E F C   F G   C
Know-ing   You, Jesus,   knowing You.
          Am Em/G F
There is no greater thing.
              C/E   F/A
You're my all, You're the best,
              C/G   F
You're my joy, my righteousness;
          C/E
And I love You,
F2/A C/G G (**Gsus** G C - *last time*)
Lord.

Verse 2   G   Am F C   F   G C
Now my heart's de- sire is to know You more,
          Am F C   Am   Gsus G
To be found in   You and known as Yours,
C C/E F G C   G/B F/A G C
To pos- sess by faith what I   could not earn,
        G/B Am F C   Am   Gsus G
All-sur-   pass- ing gift of righteous-ness.

Verse 3   G   Am F C   F G C
Oh, to know the pow'r of Your ris- en life,
          Am F C   Am Gsus G
And to know You in Your suffer- ing,
C C/E F   G C   G/B F/A G   C
To be-   come like You in Your death, my Lord,
        G/B Am F C   Am Gsus G
So with You to   live and never die.

Let Everything That Has Breath

Words and Music by
MATT REDMAN

Melody:

Let ev - 'ry - thing that,

E E/D# C#m7 A2 A2/B F#m7 B

Chorus

E   E/D#
Let everything that,   everything that,
C#m7   A2   A2/B
Everything that has breath praise the Lord.
E   E/D#
Let everything that,   everything that,
C#m7   A2   A2/B
Everything that has breath praise the Lord.

Verse 1

E   E/D#
Praise You in the morning,   praise You in the evening,
C#m7   A2
Praise You when I'm young and when I'm old.
E
Praise You when I'm laughing,
E/D#
Praise You when I'm grieving,
C#m7   A2
Praise You every season of the soul.

Pre-
Chorus

       F♯m7   **A2/B**
If we (they) could see how much You're worth,
       F♯m7   **A2/B**
Your pow'r, Your might, Your endless love,
       F♯m7   **A2/B**   **A2**   **B**
Then surely we (they) would never cease to praise.

Verse 2   **E**   **E/D♯**
      Praise You in the heavens,   joining with the angels,
  C♯m7   **A2**
      Praising You forever and a day.
  E   **E/D♯**
      Praise You on the earth now,   joining with creation,
  C♯m7   **A2**
      Calling all the nations to Your praise.

Jesus, Name Above All Names

Words and Music by
NAIDA HEARN

Melody:

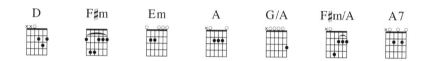

Je - sus,　name a-bove　all names,

D　　F♯m　　Em　　A　　G/A　　F♯m/A　　A7

Chorus　**D**　　　　　　**F♯m**
Jesus, name above all names,
　　　　Em　　　　**A　G/A　F♯m/A　A7**
Beautiful Savior, glorious Lord.
　　D　　　　　**F♯m**
Emmanuel, God is with us,
　　　　Em　　A7　　　**D**
Blessed Redeemer,　Living Word.

Let It Rise

Words and Music by
HOLLAND DAVIS

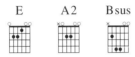

E   A2   Bsus

Verse 1
      E
Let the glory of the Lord rise among us,

Let the glory of the Lord rise among us.
      A2   **E**
Let the praises of the King rise among us, let it rise.

Verse 2
      E
Let the songs of the Lord rise among us,

Let the songs of the Lord rise among us,
      A2   **E**
Let the joy of the King rise among us, let it rise.

Chorus   **Bsus** **A2**   **E**   **Bsus** **A2**   **E**
              Oh,   let it rise. Oh,   let it rise.

Let My Words Be Few

(I'll Stand in Awe of You)

Words and Music by
MATT REDMAN
and BETH REDMAN

You are God in heav - en, ___

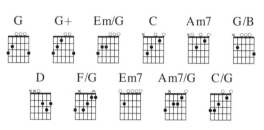

Verse 1

G   G+   Em/G   C
You are God in heaven, and here am I on earth,
G   G+   Em/G   C
So I'll let my words be few.
Am7   G/B   C   D   G
Jesus,   I am so in love with You.

Chorus

          G   F/G   Em7   Am7   Am7/G
And I'll stand in awe of You;
          G   F/G   Em7
Yes, I'll stand in awe of You.
C   Am7   Em7   C
And I'll let my words be few.
Am7   G/B   C   D   G   (C/G)
Jesus,   I am so in love with You.

Verse 2

G   G+   Em/G   C
The simplest of all love songs I want to bring to You,
G   G+   Em/G   C
So I'll let my words be few.
Am7   G/B   C   D   G
Jesus,   I am so in love with You.

Lord, I Lift Your Name on High

Words and Music by
RICK FOUNDS

Melody:

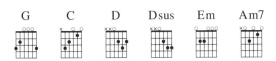

| G | C | D | Dsus | Em | Am7 |

Verse

G   C   D C
Lord, I lift Your name on high,
G   C   D   C
Lord, I love to sing Your praises.
G   C   D C
I'm so glad You're in my life.
G   C   **Dsus   D**
I'm so glad You came to save us.

Chorus

G   C   D   C   G
You came from heaven to earth to show the way,
C   D   C   G
From the earth to the cross, my debt to pay.
C   D   **Em**   **Am7**
From the cross to the grave, from the grave to the sky,
Dsus   D   G
Lord, I lift Your name on high.

Lord, Reign in Me

Words and Music by
BRENTON BROWN

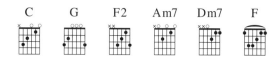

O-ver all the—— earth—— You— reign on——high,

Verse 1

    C   G   F2   G
Over all the earth You reign on high,
    C   G   F2   G
Every mountain stream, every sunset sky.
Am7   **G**   **F2**   **G** **Dm7**
But my one request, Lord, my only aim
               F   **G**
Is that You'd reign in me again.

Chorus

    C   G   F   G
Lord, reign in me, reign in Your power,
    C   G   F   G
Over all my dreams, in my darkest hour;
Am7   **G**   **F**   **G** **Dm7**
You are the Lord of all I am.
              F   **G** **C** **G** **F2** **C** **G** **F2**
So won't You reign in me again?

Verse 2
      C   G   F2   G
Over every thought, over every word,
      C   G   F2   G
May my life reflect the beauty of my Lord.
      Am7   G   F2
'Cause You mean more to me
         G   Dm7
Than any earthly thing.
             F   G
So won't You reign in me again?

Tag
             F   G   Dm7
So won't You reign in me again?
          F   G   Dm7
Won't You reign in me again?
          F   G   C
Won't You reign in me again?

Majesty

Words and Music by
JACK W. HAYFORD

Melody:

Maj-es-ty, ———— wor-ship His Maj-es-ty.

A   D/A   A7   G2/B   A7/C♯   D   A6/C♯   Bm7

D/E   E7   A/G♯   F♯m   F♯m/E   F♯m/D♯   E7sus   Dm/B

C♯+   Dm6   A/E   E/B   A/C♯   Amaj7/C♯   Cdim7   C♯

Chorus
A   D/A   A
Majesty,
A7   G2/B   A7/C♯   D   A6/C♯   Bm7
Wor- ship   His   Majesty.
D/E   E7   A
Un-   to   Jesus
    A/G♯   F♯m   F♯m/E   F♯m/D♯   E7sus   E7
Be all   glo-   ry,   honor, and praise.
A   D/A   A
Majesty,
A7   G2/B   A7/C♯   D   A6/C♯   Bm7
King-dom   au-   thority
Dm/B   C♯+   Dm6   A/E   A   E/B   A/C♯   Bm7
Flow   from His   throne un- to   His   own;
E7   D/E   E7   A   D/A   A
His an-   them raise.

Verse

Amaj7/C♯ Cdim7 Bm7
So   ex-   alt,

       E7   D/E E7   A   D/A   A
Lift up on high the name of   Jesus.

Amaj7/C♯ Cdim7 Bm7   E7
Mag-   ni-   fy, come glorify

      D/E   E7   C♯ Bm7 E7   D/E   E7
Christ Jesus,   the   King.

Tag

A   D/A   A
Majesty,

A7   G2/B   A7/C♯   D   A6/C♯   Bm7
Wor- ship   His   Majesty—

Dm/B   C♯+   Dm6   A/E   A   E/B   A/C♯   Bm7
Je-   sus   who   died, now glo- ri-   fied,

E7   D/E   E7   A   D/A   A
King of   all   kings.

Meet with Me

Words and Music by
LAMONT HIEBERT

Melody:

I'm here—— to meet—— with You,——

A/C♯   D2   E   A   F♯m7

Verse   A/C♯   D2   E   A
          I'm here to meet with You.
          A/C♯ D2   E   A
          Come and meet with me.
          A/C♯   D2   E   F♯m7
          I'm here to find You.
          A/C♯   D2   E   A
          Reveal Yourself to me.

Chorus   A/C♯ D2   E   A
          As I wait,   You make me strong.
              A/C♯ D2   E   A
          As I long,   You draw me to Your arms.
              A/C♯ D2   E   A
          As I stand   and sing Your praise,
              A/C♯   D2   E   A
          You come, You come and You fill this place.
                  A/C♯   D2
          Won't you come, won't You come
              E   A
          And fill this place?

More Love, More Power

Words and Music by
JUDE DEL HIERRO

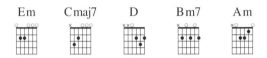

Em   Cmaj7   D   Bm7   Am

Verse **Em**   **Cmaj7**
    More love,   more power,
D   **Bm7 Em   D**
    More of You in my life.
Em   **Cmaj7**
    More love,   more power,
D   **Bm7 Em**
    More of You in my life.

Chorus **Em**   **Am**   **Em**
    And I will worship You with all of my heart,
                    Am   **Em**
    And I will worship You with all of my mind,
                    Am   **Em**
    And I will worship You with all of my strength,
                    Cmaj7   Bm7
    For You are my Lord.

Tag **Bm7**   **Cmaj7   D**   **Em**
    You are my Lord.   You are my Lord.

My Redeemer Lives

Words and Music by
REUBEN MORGAN

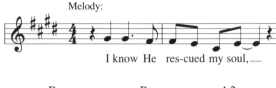

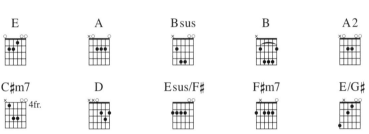

I know He res-cued my soul, —

Verse

    E   A
   I know He rescued my soul,
    E   A
   His blood, has covered my sin,
      E   A   E   A
I believe,   I believe.
    E   A
   My shame, He's taken away,
    E   A
   My pain is healed in His name.
      E   A   E   A
I believe,   I believe.
Bsus   **B**
   I'll raise a banner
A   B
  'Cause my Lord has conquered the grave!

Chorus   **E**   **A2**   **C♯m7** **B**
My Redeemer lives! My Redeemer lives!
                  E   **A2**   **C♯m7** **B**
My Redeemer lives! My Redeemer lives!

Bridge   **D**   **Esus/F♯**
You lift my burden   and I rise with You.
           E   **F♯m7**   **E/G♯**   **B**
I'm dancing on this mountaintop to see Your kingdom come.

No Other Gods

Words and Music by
DAVID MOFFITT

Melody:

The God of the heav - ens,

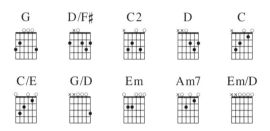

Verse 1

   G   **D/F♯**
The God of the heavens, the Ancient of Days,
   C2   **D**
The God of our fathers, and God of my praise.
   G   **D/F♯**
The Alpha, Omega, Beginning and End,
   C2   **D**
For ever and ever Your Kingdom will stand.
C   **D**   **C/E**
  We come to bow before You now.
   G/D
We come to lay our lives down.

Chorus   **G**
We will have no other gods before You.
Em
Nothing on earth will compete for Your throne.
C2   **Am7**
You are the sovereign I Am,
                     Em/D   **D**
And You'll reign in our hearts   alone.
G
We will exalt You on high forever,
Em
King of all kings and the Lord of all lords.
C   **G/D**   **G**
We will have no other gods before You.

Verse 2   **G**   **D/F♯**
Our Maker, Creator, before time began,
     C2   **D**
Messiah and Savior, Redeemer and Friend.
     G   **D/F♯**
Our Rock of salvation, so faithful and true,
     C2   **D**
We give all the glory and honor to You.
C   **D**   **C/E**   **G/D**
For You alone are worthy of our never-ending love.

O Praise Him
(All This for a King)

Words and Music by
DAVID CROWDER

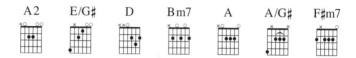

Verse 1

    A2   **E/G♯**   **D**
Turn your ear to heaven and hear the noise inside,
    A2
The sound of angel's awe,
    E/G♯   **D**
The sound of angel's songs, and all this for a King.
Bm7   **D**
We could join and sing all to Christ the King.

Pre-Chorus 1

    E/G♯   **D**
How constant, how   divine,
    E/G♯   **D**
This song of ours   will rise.
    E/G♯   **D**
O how constant, how   divine,
    E/G♯   **D**
This love of ours   will rise, will rise.

Chorus 1   **A**   **A/G♯**
               O praise Him, O praise Him;
               F♯m7   **D**   **Bm7**   **A**
               He is holy, He is ho-   ly, yeah.

Verse 2   **A2**   **E/G♯**   **D**
               Turn your gaze to heaven and raise a joyous noise,
                     A2
               The sound of salvation come,
                     E/G♯   **D**
               The sound of rescued ones, and all this for a King.
               Bm7   **D**
               Angels join to sing all for Christ the King.

Pre-   **E/G♯**   **D**
Chorus 2   How infinite   and sweet,
               E/G♯   **D**
                   This love so res-   cuing.
               E/G♯   **D**
               O how infinite-   ly sweet,
               E/G♯   **D**
               This great love that has   redeemed. As one we sing.

Chorus 2   **A**   **A/G♯**
               Alleluia! Alleluia!
               F♯m7   **D**   **Bm7**   **A**
               He is holy, He is ho-   ly, yeah.

Once Again

Words and Music by
MATT REDMAN

Je-sus Christ,— I think up-on Your sac-ri-fice;

D A/D G/D G D/F♯ Asus

A D2 Dsus G2 Bm G/B

Verse 1
   D   A/D   G/D   D
Jesus Christ, I think upon Your sacrifice;
G   D/F♯   G   Asus   A
You became nothing, poured out to death.
D   A/D   G/D   D
Many times I've wondered at Your gift of life,
   G   Asus   A   D   D2   D
And I'm in that place once a-   gain.
G   Asus   A   D   Dsus
I'm in that place once a-   gain.

Chorus
   D/F♯   G2   D/F♯   Asus   A
Once again I look upon the cross where You died.
      D/F♯   G2   D/F♯   Asus   A
I'm humbled by Your mercy and I'm broken inside.
Bm   G
Once again I thank You,
D/F♯   A   G/B   Asus   A   D
Once again I pour out my life.

Verse 2   **D**   **A/D** **G/D**   **D**

               Now You are exalted to the highest place,

               G   **D/F♯**   **G**   **Asus**   **A**

               King of the heavens, where one day I'll bow.

               D   **A/D** **G/D**   **D**

               But, for now, I marvel at this saving grace,

                  G   **Asus**   **A** **D** **D2** **D**

               And I'm full of praise once a-   gain.

               G   **Asus**   **A** **D** **Dsus**

               I'm full of praise once a-   gain.

Bridge   **G**   **Asus**   **A** **D/F♯**

               Thank You for the cross,   Thank You for the cross,

               G   **Asus**   **A** **D**

               Thank You for the cross, my Friend.

Only a God Like You

Words and Music by
TOMMY WALKER

Melody:

For the prais - es___ of man, ___

G   D   Em   C   C2   Dsus   Bm7

Em7   Am7   G/B   B7(♭9)   D/G   G/D   C/E

Verse

         G   **D**   **Em**   **C**

For the praises of man, I will never, ever stand;

         G   **D**

For the kingdoms of this world,

         C2   **Dsus**   **D**

I'll never give my heart away or shout my praise;

        G   **D**

My allegiance and devotion,

           Em   **C**

My heart's desire and all emotion,

        G   **D**   **C2** **D** **Dsus**

Go to serve the Man who died upon that tree.

Chorus 1   **G**   **D** **Bm7**

        Only a God like You

        Em7   **C**

Could be worthy of my praise, and all my hope and faith;

     G   **D** **Bm7**

To only a King of all kings,

      Em7   **C**

Do I bow my knee and sing, give my everything;

Chorus 2

Am7   G/B   C   Em7
To only my Maker, my Father, my Savior,

Am7   G/B   C   Em7
Redeemer, Restorer, Rebuilder, Rewarder;

Am7 C   Dsus
To only a God like You,

D   G D Em C (G D Em C G)
Do I give my praise.

Bridge   **G   D**
Only the God, who left His throne above,

Em   C
He came to live with us, came to be one of us;

G   D
To only the One, who stopped to heal that blind man,

Em   C
Took the time to save that one lost lamb;

G   D
To only the King, who wore that crown of thorns

B7(♭9)   Em   C
So   I could wear the crown of life;

G   D
And to only the One, who conquered sin and death

Em
So we could be set free,

C2
So we could stand here and sing.

Tag   **G   D/G D   G/D Em7**
Only a God like You,   only a God like You,

C/E C
Only a God like You.

More Precious Than Silver

Words and Music by
LYNN DE SHAZO

Lord, You are more pre - cious

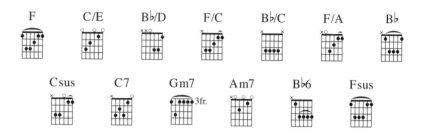

F   C/E   B♭/D   F/C   B♭/C   F/A   B♭

Csus   C7   Gm7   Am7   B♭6   Fsus

Chorus

F	C/E	B♭/D		F/C B♭/C

Lord, You are more precious than silver;

F   **C/E** **F/A** **B♭**   **Csus** **C7**

Lord, You are   more costly than gold.

F   **C/E** **B♭/D**   **F/C**

Lord, You are more beautiful than diamonds,

Gm7 **Am7** **B♭6**   **B♭/C** **C7** **Fsus** **F**

And nothing I   desire compares   with You.

Open Our Eyes

Words and Music by
BOB CULL

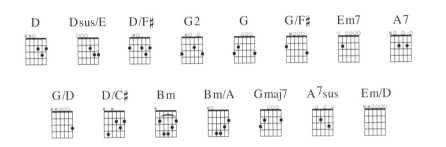

D Dsus/E D/F♯ G2 G G/F♯ Em7 A7

G/D D/C♯ Bm Bm/A Gmaj7 A7sus Em/D

Chorus

D Dsus/E D/F♯ G2 G G/F♯ Em7
O- pen   our   eyes, Lord,

A7   G/D D D/C♯ Bm
We want to see Je-   sus,

Bm/A   Gmaj7 Em7 A7sus
To reach out and touch   Him,

A7   G/D D
And say that we love   Him.

D Dsus/E D/F♯ G2 G G/F♯ Em7
O- pen   our   ears, Lord,

A7   G/D D D/C♯ Bm
And help us to lis-   ten.

Bm/A Gmaj7 Em7 A7sus
Open our eyes,   Lord,

A7   Em/D D
We want to see Je-   sus.

Open the Eyes of My Heart

Words and Music by
PAUL BALOCHE

Melody:

O-pen the eyes of my heart, Lord;

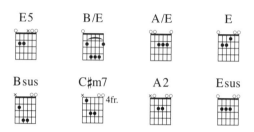

E5   B/E   A/E   E

Bsus   C#m7   A2   Esus

Chorus

E5   **B/E**
Open the eyes of my heart, Lord; open the eyes of my heart.
          A/E   **E**
I want to see You, I want to see You.

Verse

                    Bsus   **C#m7**
To see You high and lifted up,
A2   **Bsus**
Shining in the light of Your glory.
                    C#m7   **A2**   **Bsus**
Pour out Your pow'r and love as we sing holy, holy, holy.

Bridge

E5   **B/E**
Holy, holy, holy. Holy, holy, holy.
A/E   **E**   **Esus**
Holy, holy, holy. I want to see You.

Tag

              E   **Esus**   **E**
I want to see You.   I want to see You.

Refiner's Fire

Words and Music by
BRIAN DOERKSEN

Pu - ri - fy —— my heart, ——

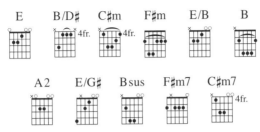

Verse 1

E B/D♯ C♯m   F♯m
Purify my heart, let me be as gold
      E/B B E/B B
And pre- cious sil-   ver;
E B/D♯ C♯m   F♯m   E/B B
Purify my heart, let me be as gold, pure   gold.

Chorus

E A2   B   E   A2   B
Re- finer's fire, my heart's one desire
       E   B   E   A2   B
Is to be holy, set apart for You, Lord.
           E   B   E/G♯ A2   Bsus   B
I choose to be holy, set   apart for You, my Master,
F♯m7   B   C♯m7 B/D♯ E
Ready to do Your will.

Verse 2

E B/D♯ C♯m   F♯m
Purify my heart, cleanse me from within
      E/B B E/B B
And make me ho- ly;
E B/D♯ C♯m   F♯m E/B B
Purify my heart, cleanse me from my sin deep within.

Rock of Ages

Words and Music by
RITA BALOCHE

Melody:

There is no rock, there is no god ___ like our ___ God.

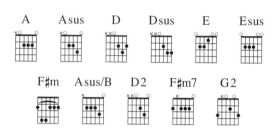

A Asus D Dsus E Esus

F#m Asus/B D2 F#m7 G2

Verse

A   Asus
There is no rock,

A   Asus A Asus A Asus
There is no god like our God.

D   Dsus D   Dsus A Asus A Asus
No other name worthy of all our praise.

  E   Esus E   Esus
The Rock of Salvation that cannot be moved,

  F#m   D
He's proven Himself to be faithful and true.

Asus/B   D2   A Asus A (Asus)
There is no rock, there is no god like ours.

Chorus

      F#m7 D A   E
Rock of a- ges, Jesus is the Rock.

      F#m7 D A   E
Rock of a- ges, Jesus is the Rock.

      F#m7 D A   E
Rock of a- ges, Jesus is the Rock.

G2   D   A Asus A (Asus)
There is no rock, there is no god like ours.

Sanctuary

Words and Music by
JOHN W. THOMPSON
and RANDY SCRUGGS

Melody:

Lord, pre - pare me to be a sanc - tu - ar - y,

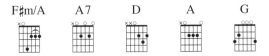

F#m/A   A7   D   A   G

Chorus   **F#m/A   A7   D   A**
Lord,   pre- pare me to be a sanctuary,
               G   D   A
Pure and holy, tried and true;
F#m/A   A7   D   A
With   thanks-giving, I'll be a living
             G   A7   D
Sanctuary for   You.

Shine, Jesus, Shine

Words and Music by
GRAHAM KENDRICK

Lord, the light of Your love is shin-ing,

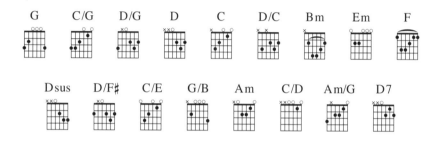

Verse 1

G   C/G   G   D/G
Lord, the light of Your love is shining,

G   C/G   G   D
In the midst of the darkness shining;

C   D/C   Bm   Em
Jesus, Light of the world, shine upon us,

C   D/C   Bm   Em
Set us free by the truth You now bring us;

F   Dsus D F   Dsus   D
Shine on me,   Shine on me.

Chorus   **G**   **D/F♯** **C/E**
Shine, Jesus, shine,
C **G/B** **Am**   **C/D** **D**   **C/E** **D/F♯**
Fill this   land with the Fa-   ther's glo- ry.
G   **D/F♯** **C/E** **C** **G/B** **Am** **Am/G** **F** **D/F♯** **D**
Blaze, Spirit blaze; set our   hearts on   fire.
G   **D/F♯** **C/E**
Flow, river,   flow,
C **G/B** **Am**   **C/D** **D** **C/E** **D/F♯**
Flood the   nations with grace and mer- cy.
G   **D/F♯**   **C/E** **C**   **G/B** **Am** **D7**   **G**
Send forth Your Word, Lord, and   let   there be light.

Verse 2   **G**   **C/G**   **G**   **D/G**
Lord, I come to Your awesome presence,
G   **C/G**   **G**   **D**
From the shadows into Your radiance;
C   **D/C**   **Bm**   **Em**
By the blood I may enter Your brightness;
C   **D/C**   **Bm**   **Em**
Search me, try me, consume all my darkness;
F   **Dsus** **D** **F**   **Dsus** **D**
Shine on me,   Shine on me.

Verse 3   **G**   **C/G**   **G**   **D/G**
As we gaze on Your kingly brightness
G   **C/G** **G**   **D**
So our faces display Your likeness,
C   **D/C**   **Bm**   **Em**
Ever changing from glory to glory;
C   **D/C**   **Bm**   **Em**
Mirrored here, may our lives tell Your story;
F   **Dsus** **D** **F**   **Dsus** **D**
Shine on me,   Shine on me.

Shout to the Lord

Words and Music by
DARLENE ZSCHECH

My Je - sus, my Sav - ior,

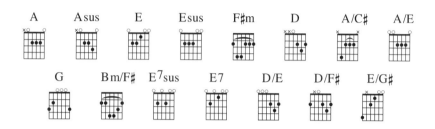

Verse

	A	Asus	A	E	Esus	E

 My Je- sus, my Sav- ior,

F♯m   **E**   **D**
Lord, there is none like You;

     A/C♯   **D**   **A/E**
All of my days,   I want to praise

     F♯m   **G**   **Bm/F♯**   **E7sus**   **E7**
The wonders of Your might-y   love.

A   **Asus**   **A**   **E**   **Esus**   **E**
 My com- fort, my shel- ter,

F♯m   **E**   **D**
Tower of refuge and strength;

     A/C♯   **D**   **A/E**
Let every breath, all that I am,

F♯m   **G**   **Bm/F♯**   **E7sus**   **E7**
Never cease to wor-ship   You!

Chorus   A   F♯m   D   D/E   E

Shout to the Lord, all the earth, let us sing,

A   F♯m   D   E7sus   E7

Power and majesty, Praise to the King;

F♯m   E   D

Mountains bow down and the seas will roar

       E   D/F♯   E/G♯   E7

At the sound of Your name.

A   F♯m   D   D/E   E

I sing for joy at the work of Your hands;

   A   F♯m   D   E7sus   E7

Forever I'll love You, forever I'll stand!

F♯m   E   D   E   A

Nothing compares to the promise I have in   You.

Shout to the North

Words and Music by
MARTIN SMITH

Melody:

Men of faith, rise up and sing

G D C Em G/B Dsus

Verse 1

       G   **D**   **C**   **G**   **D**   **C**
Men of faith, rise up and sing of the great and glorious King.

       G   **D**   **C**
You are strong when you feel weak,

       G   **D**   **C**
In your broken-ness complete.

Chorus **G**   **C**   **D** **G**   **C**   **D**
Shout to the north and the south; sing to the east and the west.

Em **G** **C**   **D** **C**   **D**   **G**
Je-   sus is Savior to all, Lord of heaven and earth.

Verse 2

       G   **D**   **C**   **G**   **D**   **C**
Rise up, women of the truth, stand and sing to broken hearts

       G   **D**   **C**
Who can know the healing pow'r

       G   **D**   **C**
Of our awesome King of love.

Verse 3

          G   **D**   **C**
Rise up, church with broken wings,

          G   **D**   **C**
Fill this place with songs again

          G   **D**   **C**
Of our God who reigns on high.

          G   **D**   **C**
By His grace again we'll fly.

Bridge   **Em**   **C**
We've been through fire, we've been through rain;

        Em   **C**
We've been refined by the pow'r of His name.

        Em   **C**
We've fallen deeper in love with You.

                 G/B   **Dsus** **D**
You've burned the truth on our lips.

Tag   **C**   **D**   **G**   **C**   **D**   **G**
Lord of heaven and earth, Lord of heaven and earth.

Sing to the King

Words and Music by
BILLY FOOTE,
CHARLES SILVERSTER
and HORNE

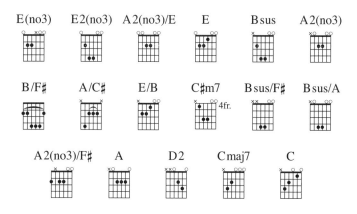

Verse 1

E(no3)   E2(no3)   A2(no3)/E   E
Sing to the King who is coming   to   reign.
E(no3)   Bsus   A2(no3)   E
Glory to Jesus, the Lamb that was slain.
                 B/F♯   A/C♯   E/B
Life and salvation His empire shall bring,
C♯m7   Bsus/F♯   Bsus/A   E(no3)
Joy to the nations when Jesus is   King.

Chorus   **E**
Come, let us sing a song,
   A2(no3)/F♯   **A**
A song declaring we belong to Jesus.
        E   **D2** **A**
He's all we need.
E
Lift up a heart of praise.
A2(no3)/F♯   **A**
Sing now with voices raised to Jesus;
           E(no3)
Sing to the King.

Verse 2   **E(no3)**   **E2(no3)**   **A2(no3)/E**   **E**
For His returning we watch and we pray.
E(no3)   **Bsus**   **A2(no3)**   **E**
We will be ready the dawn of that day.
          B/F♯   **A/C♯**   **E/B**
We'll join in singing with all the redeemed.
C♯m7 **Bsus/F♯**   **Bsus/A** **E(no3)**
Satan is vanquished, and Jesus is   King.

Bridge   **D2**   **A**   **E**
Sing to the King. Sing to   the King.
         Bsus   **D2** **A/C♯**   **Cmaj7**   **C**
Sing to the King.   Sing to the   King.

Sometimes by Step

Words and Music by
RICH MULLINS
and DAVID STRASSER

Melody:

Some - times the night

G   D/G   C2/E   Dsus   D   Bm

C   Em   Am7   D/F♯   C/E   D⁷sus

D7   C/G   Am   F   C2   G/D

Verse 1

G   D/G
Sometimes the night was beautiful,
G   D/G
Sometimes the sky was so far away,
C2/E   Dsus   D
    Sometimes it seemed steep, so close you could touch it,
                    Bm
But your heart would break.
                    C   Bm
Sometimes the morning came too soon,
                    C   Em
Sometimes the day could be so hot.
            Dsus   C
There was so much work left to do,
                    Am7
But so much you'd already done.

Chorus   G   D/F♯   D   C/E   D7sus   D7   G

O God, You are my God,   and I will ever   praise You.

          G   D/F♯   D   C/E   D7sus   D7   G

O God, You are my God,   and I will ever   praise You.

                Em   Dsus   D

I will seek You in the morning,

                   C   Am7

And I will learn to walk in Your ways;

              G   D/F♯   D

And step by step You'll lead me,

                 C/E   D7sus   D7   G   (C/G   D)

And I will follow You all   of   my   days.

Verse 2   G   D/G

Sometimes I think of Abraham,

G   D/G

How one star he saw had been lit from me.

C2/E Dsus   D   Bm

He was a stranger in this land, and I am that no less than he.

C   Bm

And on this road to righteousness,

C   Em

Sometimes the climb can be so steep.

Dsus   C   Am7

I may falter in my steps, but never beyond Your reach.

Tag   Em   Dsus   D

And I will follow You all of my days,

                Am   F   C2

And I will follow You all of my days.

            G/D   D

And step by step You'll lead me,

               C/E   D7sus   D7   G

And I will follow You all   of   my   days.

Step by Step

Words and Music by
DAVID STRASSER

Melody:

O God, You are my God,

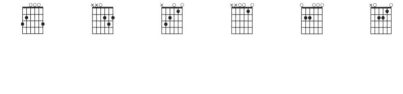

G   D   C   C/D   Em   Am

Pre-
Chorus

     G   **D**   **C**   **C/D**   **G**
O God, You are my God, and I will ever praise You.
     G   **D**   **C**   **C/D**   **G**
O God, You are my God, and I will ever praise You.

Chorus

       Em   **D**
I will seek You in the morning,
           C   **Am**
And I will learn to walk in Your ways;
        G   **D**
And step by step You'll lead me,
        C   **C/D**   **G**
And I will follow You all of my days.

Take My Life

Words and Music by
SCOTT UNDERWOOD

Melody:

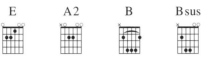

Ho - li - ness, ___ ho - li - ness

E   A2   B   B sus

Verse 1
    E   A2   B   A2
    Holiness, holiness is what I long for;
    E   A2   B   A2
    Holiness is what I need.
    E   A2   B   A2   E A2 B A2
    Holiness, holiness is what You want from me.

Verse 2
    E   A2   B   A2
    Faithfulness, faithfulness is what I long for;
    E   A2   B   A2
    Faithfulness is what I need.
    E   A2   B
    Faithfulness, faithfulness
                 A2   E A2 B Bsus
    Is what You want from me.

Chorus
    B   E A2   B   A2
    Take my heart   and form it;
              E A2   B   A2
    Take my mind – transform it;
              E A2 B   A2   E   A2   B   A2
    Take my will –   conform it   To Yours, to Yours, O Lord.

Tag
         E   A2   B
    To Yours, to Yours, O Lord.

Additional verses: Righteousness ... Purity ... etc.

That's Why We Praise Him

Words and Music by
TOMMY WALKER

Melody:

He came to— live, live a per-fect life;

Chord diagrams: C | G | F | G/F | Dm

C/E | Dm/F | Gsus | Am | G/B

Verse 1

    C G F
He came to live, live a perfect life;
    C G   F
He came to be the Living Word, our light.
    C G   F
He came to die so we'd be reconciled;
    C G   F G/F F G
He came to rise to show His pow'r and might.

Chorus

 C   G   F
That's why we praise Him, that's why we sing;
 C   G   F G/F F G
That's why we offer Him our ev-'ry- thing.
 C   G   F
That's why we bow down and worship this King,
    Dm C/E Dm/F Gsus Am
'Cause He gave His ev-   'rything,
    Dm C/E Dm/F Gsus C
'Cause He gave His ev-   'rything.

Verse 2

              C   G   F
He came to live,   live again in us;
              C G   F
He came to be   our conqu'ring King and Friend.
              C G   F
He came to heal   and show the lost ones His love;
              C G   F   G/F F G
He came to go   prepare a place for   us.

Bridge   **C   G/B F   G C   G/B F   G**
            Halle,   hallelujah.   Halle,   hallelujah.

The Heart of Worship

Words and Music by
MATT REDMAN

Melody:

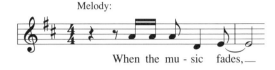

When the mu - sic fades, —

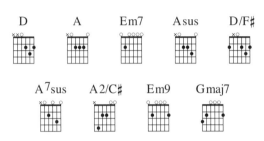

D   A   Em7   Asus   D/F♯

A⁷sus   A2/C♯   Em9   Gmaj7

Verse 1

D   A   Em7
  When the music fades, all is stripped away,
                   Asus   A
And I simply come;
D   A   Em7
  Longing just to bring something that's of worth
                  Asus   A
That will bless Your heart.

**Pre-
Chorus**

Em7   D/F♯   A7sus
  I'll bring You more than a song, for a song in itself
Em7   D/F♯   A7sus
  Is not what You have required.
Em7   D/F♯   A7sus
  You search much deeper within

Through the way things appear;
Em7   D/F♯   Asus   A
  You're looking into my heart.

Chorus   **D**   **A2/C♯**

I'm coming back to the heart of worship,

       Em9   **D/F♯**   **Gmaj7** **A7sus**

It's all about You, it's all about You, Jesus.

     D   **A2/C♯**

I'm sorry, Lord, for the thing I've made it,

          Em9   **D/F♯**   **Gmaj7** **A7sus**   **D**

When it's all about You,   all about You,   Jesus.

Verse 2   **D**   **A**   **Em7**

King of endless worth, no one could express

                 Asus   **A**

How much You deserve.

     D   **A**   **Em7**

Though I'm weak and poor, all I have is Yours,

             Asus   **A**

Every single breath.

The Potter's Hand

Words and Music by
DARLENE ZSCHECH

Melody:

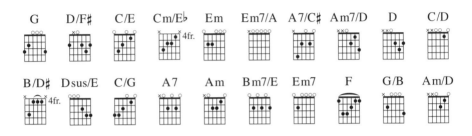

Beau-ti-ful Lord,— won-der-ful Sav - ior,

G   D/F♯   C/E   Cm/E♭   Em   Em7/A   A7/C♯   Am7/D   D   C/D

B/D♯   Dsus/E   C/G   A7   Am   Bm7/E   Em7   F   G/B   Am/D

Verse 1

G   D/F♯
Beautiful Lord, wonderful Savior,
C/E   Cm/E♭
I know for sure all of my days are
Em   Em7/A   A7/C♯ Am7/D   D   C/D
Held in Your hand, Crafted into Your perfect   plan.

Verse 2

G   D/F♯
You gently call me into Your presence
C/E   Cm/E♭
Guiding me by Your Holy Spirit.
Em
Teach me, dear Lord,
        Em7/A   A7/C♯   Am7/D   D   B/D♯
To live all of my life   through Your eyes.

Pre-
Chorus

Em   **D**   **Dsus/E** **D/F♯**
I'm captured by Your holy call-   ing,
G   **C/G**   **G**   **D/F♯** **Em**
Set me apart, I know You're draw-ing   me to Yourself;
Em7/A **A7**   **Am7/D** **D**
Lead me, Lord, I pray.

Chorus

G   **D/F♯**   **Am**   **Bm7/E** **Em7**
Take me, mold me, use me, fill   me;
  F   **C/E** **Am** **G/B** **Am** **Am7/D** **D**
I give my life to the Pot- ter's   hand.
G   **D/F♯**   **Am**   **Bm7/E** **Em7**
Call me, guide me, lead me, walk beside   me;
  F   **C/E** **Am** **G/B** **Am** **G/B** **C/D**
I give my life to the Pot- ter's   hand.

Tag

(*last time -* **F**   **C/E** **Am/D** **C/D** **G**)
    I give my life to the Pot-   ter's hand.

The Power of Your Love

Words and Music by
GEOFF BULLOCK

Melody:

Lord, I come to You,

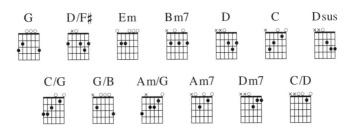

Verse 1

    G   D/F♯   Em   Bm7   Em

Lord, I come to You, let my heart be changed, renewed,

    D   C

Flowing from the grace

    Dsus D Em Dsus D

That I've found in You;

    G   D/F♯   Em

And Lord, I've come to know

    Bm7   Em

The weaknesses I see in me

    D   C Dsus

Will be stripped away

                  C/G G G/B

By the pow'r of Your love.

Chorus C   Em   D   Am/G   G   Em   D
Hold   me close, let Your love surround   me,
C   Em   D
Bring   me near,
          G   Am7   G/B   Dm7   G
Draw me to Your side;
    C   Em   D   Am/G   G
And as   I wait I'll rise up like the ea-   gle,
          D/F♯   Em
And I will soar with You,
          D   C   C/D   C/G   G
Your Spirit leads me on in the pow'r of Your love.

Verse 2 G   D/F♯   Em   Bm7   Em
          Lord, unveil my eyes, let me see You, face to face,
                    D   C
The knowledge of Your love,
          Dsus   D   Em   Dsus   D
As You live   in   me;
G   D/F♯   Em
    And Lord, renew my mind,
          Bm7   Em
As Your will unfolds in my life,
          D   C   Dsus
In living ev'ry day
                    C/G   G   G/B
By the pow'r of Your love.

The Wonderful Cross

Words by ISAAC WATTS
Music by LOWELL MASON
additional material by CHRIS TOMLIN,
J.D. WALT, and JESSE REEVES

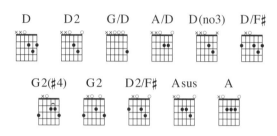

Verse 1

D	D2	D	D2	D	G/D	D	D2	D

When I sur- vey the   won- drous   cross

D		G/D	D	D2	D	A/D	D	D2

On which the Prince of   Glo-ry   died,

D	D2	D	D2	D	G/D	D	D2	D

My richest gain I   count but   loss,

D2	D	D2	D	D2	D(no3)

And pour contempt on all my   pride.

Verse 2

D	D2	D	D2	D	G/D	D	D2	D

See, from His head, His   hands, His   feet,

D		G/D	D	D2	D	A/D	D	D2

Sorrow and love flow   min-gled   down.

D	D2	D	D2	D	G/D	D	D2	D

Did e'er such love and   sor- row   meet,

D2	D	D2	D	D2	D

Or thorns compose so rich a   crown?

Chorus   **D/F♯**   **G2(♯4)**   **G2**   **D2/F♯**

Oh, the won-   derful cross,

            D/F♯   **G2(♯4)**   **G2**   **D2/F♯**

Oh, the won-   derful cross

            D/F♯   **G2(♯4)**   **G2**

Bids me come and die

                 D2/F♯   **D/F♯** **Asus**   **A**

And find that I may   truly live.

            D/F♯   **G2(♯4)**   **G2**   **D2/F♯**

Oh, the won-   derful cross,

            D/F♯   **G2(♯4)**   **G2**   **D2/F♯**

Oh, the won-   derful cross,

            D/F♯   **G2**   **D/F♯**

All who gather here by grace draw near

               Asus   **A** **(D)**

And bless Your name.

Verse 3   **D**   **D2**   **D**   **D2**   **D** **G/D** **D** **D2** **D**

Were the whole realm of   na-   ture   mine,

           D   **G/D** **D** **D2** **D** **A/D** **D**   **D2**

That were an of-   f'ring   far too   small.

           D   **D2**   **D**   **D2**   **D** **G/D** **D** **D2** **D**

Love so a-   maz-ing,   so   di-   vine,

                 D2 **D** **D2** **D** **D2** **D**

Demands my soul, my life, my   all!

Trading My Sorrows

Words and Music by
DARRELL EVANS

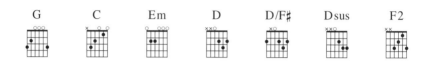

G	C	Em	D	D/F♯	D sus	F2

Chorus

G   C   Em   D   G   C   Em   D
I'm trading my sor-   rows,   I'm trading my shame,
G   C   Em   D   G C Em   D
I'm laying them down for the joy of the Lord.
G   C   Em   D   G   C   Em   D
I'm trading my sick-   ness,   I'm trading my pain,
G   C   Em   D   G C Em   D
I'm laying them down for the joy of the Lord.

Channel

G   C   Em   D
Yes, Lord, yes, Lord, yes, yes, Lord;
G   C   Em   D/F♯
Yes, Lord, yes, Lord, yes, yes, Lord;
G   C   Em   D   G C Em   D
Yes, Lord, yes, Lord, yes, yes, Lord, Amen.

Verse   **G**   **C**   **Em**   **D**

I am pressed but not crushed, persecuted, not abandoned,

G   **C**   **Em**   **D**

  Struck down, but not destroyed;

    G   **C**   **Em**   **D**

I am blessed beyond the curse, for His promise will endure,

      G   **C**   **Em**   **D**

That His joy's gonna be my strength.

D   **Dsus** **D**

  Though the sorrow may last for the night,

  F2   **C**

His joy comes in the morning.

Tag   **G**   **C**   **Em**   **D**

Lai, lai, lai, lai, lai, lai, lai, lai, lai, lai, lai;

    G   **C**   **Em**   **D**

Lai, lai, lai, lai, lai, lai, lai, lai, lai, lai, lai;

    G   **C**

Lai, lai, lai, lai, lai, lai, lai,

Em   **D**   **G** **C** **Em** **D** **(G)**

Lai, lai, lai, lai, lai, lai.

We Bow Down

Words and Music by
TWILA PARIS

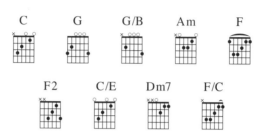

Verse 1

     C   G   C
You are Lord of creation and Lord of my life,
           G
Lord of the land and the sea.
     C   G/B   Am
You were Lord of the heavens before there was time,
    F   G   C
And Lord of all lords You will be!

Chorus 1

     F2 C/E   G   C
We bow down, and we worship You, Lord.
     F2 C/E   G   C
We bow down, and we worship You, Lord.
     F2 C/E   G   Am
We bow down, and we worship You, Lord.
Dm7   G   C F/C C
Lord of all lords You will be!

Verse 2   **C**   **G**   **C**

       You are King of creation and King of my life,

                          G

       King of the land and the sea.

             C   **G/B**   **Am**

       You were King of the heavens before there was time,

        F   **G**   **C**

       And King of all kings You will be!

Chorus 2   **F2**   **C/E**   **G**   **C**

       We bow down,   and we crown You the King.

                F2   **C/E**   **G**   **C**

       We bow down,   and we crown You the King.

                F2   **C/E**   **G**   **Am**

       We bow down,   and we crown You the King.

       Dm7   **G**   **C**   **F/C**   **C**

       King of all kings You will be!

There Is None Like You

Words and Music by
LENNY LEBLANC

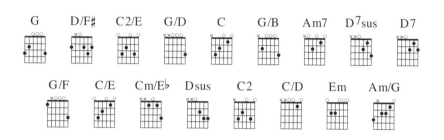

Chorus
    G   D/F♯   C2/E G/D
       There is none like You;
    C   G/B   Am7   D7sus D7
       No one else can touch my heart like You do.
    G   D/F♯   G/F   C/E Cm/E♭
       I could search for all eternity long   and find
    G/D   Dsus   D7sus D7 G (G/B)
       There is none   like   You.

Verse
         C2   C/D   G   D/F♯ Em
       Your mercy flows like a river wide
         Am7   D/F♯   G G/B
       And healing comes from Your hands;
         C2   C/D   G   Em
       Suffering children are safe in Your arms,
         Am7   Am/G D/F♯ C/E D/F♯
       There is none like You.

We Bring the Sacrifice of Praise

Words and Music by
KIRK DEARMAN

Melody:

We bring the sac-ri-fice of praise

D	Em7(11)	D/F♯	D7	G	Em7

A7	F♯m7	Bm7	Gmaj7/A	C/D	G/A

Chorus

D   Em7(11)   D/F♯   D7
We bring the sacrifice of praise
         G   D/F♯   Em7   A7
Into the house of the Lord;
D   Em7(11)   F♯m7   Bm7
We bring the sacrifice of praise
         Em7   Gmaj7/A   A7   D   C/D
Into the house   of   the   Lord.
D7   G   F♯m7   Bm7
And we offer up to You
         Em7   G/A   A7   D   Em7   D/F♯
The sacrific-   es   of   thanks-giv-   ing;
D7   G   Em7   F♯m7   Bm7
And we offer up to You
         Em7   G/A   A7   D
The sacrific-   es   of   joy.

We Want to See Jesus Lifted High

Words and Music by
DOUG HORLEY

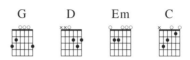

We want to see Je - sus lift - ed high, ____

Verse

G   D   Em
We want to see Jesus lifted high,
        C   G
A banner that flies across this land,
           D   Em
That all men might see the truth and know
        C
He is the way to heaven.

Chorus 1 G   D
    We want to see, we want to see,
 Em   C   G
    We want to see Jesus lifted high.
        D
We want to see, we want to see,
 Em   C   G
    We want to see Jesus lifted high.

Bridge   **D**   **Em**

Step by step we're moving forward,

            D   **Em**

Little by little taking ground.

          D   **Em**

Every prayer a powerful weapon,

               C

Strongholds come tumbling

D

Down, and down, and down, and down.

Chorus 2   **G**   **D**

  We're gonna see,   we're gonna see,

Em   **C**   **G**

  We're gonna see Jesus lifted high.

             D

We're gonna see,   we're gonna see,

Em   **C**   **G**

  We're gonna see Jesus lifted high.

We Will Glorify

Words and Music by
TWILA PARIS

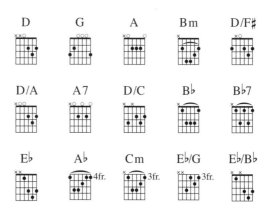

Verse 1

    D   **G**   **A**   **D**
We will glori-fy the King of kings,

    G   **A**   **D**
We will glori-fy the Lamb;

    G   **A**   **Bm**
We will glori-fy the Lord of lords,

D/F♯ **G**   **D/A** **A7** **D**
Who is the great   I   AM.

Verse 2   **G**   **A**   **D**
Lord Jehovah reigns in majesty,
           G   **A**   **D**
We will bow before His throne;
           G   **A**   **Bm**
We will worship Him in righteousness,
D/F♯   **G**   **D/A**   **A7**   **D**
We will worship Him   a-   lone.
D/C   **B♭**   **B♭7** - *modulation*

Verse 3   **E♭**   **A♭**   **B♭**   **E♭**
He is Lord of heaven, Lord of earth,
           A♭   **B♭**   **E♭**
He is Lord of all who live;
           A♭   **B♭**   **Cm**
He is Lord above the universe,
E♭/G   **A♭**   **E♭/B♭**   **B♭7**   **E♭**
All   praise to Him   we   give.

Verse 4   **A♭**   **B♭**   **E♭**
Hallelujah   to the King of kings,
          A♭   **B♭**   **E♭**
Hallelujah to the Lamb;
          A♭   **B♭**   **Cm**
Hallelujah to the Lord of lords,
E♭/G   **A♭**   **E♭/B♭**   **B♭7**   **E♭**
Who   is the great   I   AM.

Worthy Is the Lamb

Words and Music by
DARLENE ZSCHECH

Melody:

Thank You for the cross, —— Lord.

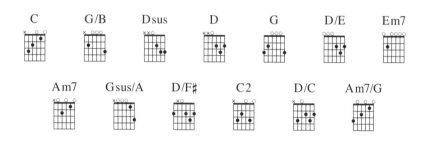

C   G/B   Dsus   D   G   D/E   Em7

Am7   Gsus/A   D/F♯   C2   D/C   Am7/G

Verse

                    C   **G/B**
Thank You for the cross, Lord.
                    C   **Dsus** **D** **G**
Thank You for the price You   paid.
                    D/E   **Em7**
Bearing all my sin and shame,
           D   **C**   **Am7** **G/B** **Dsus** **D**
In love You came and gave   amazing grace.
G   **Gsus/A** **G/B**   **C**   **G/B**
Thank You   for this love, Lord.
                    C **Dsus** **D** **G**
Thank You for the nail-pierced   hands.
                    D/E   **Em7**
Washed me in Your cleansing flow,
           D   **C**   **Am7** **G/B** **Dsus** **D/F♯**
Now all I know, Your forgiveness and embrace.

Chorus   **G**   **D/F♯** **Am7** **G/B** **C2** **C**

Worthy is the Lamb, seated on the throne.

D   **D/C**   **G/B** **C**

Crown You now with many crowns,

    Am7   **Am7/G** **D** **D/F♯**

You reign victori-   ous.

G   **D/F♯** **Am7** **G/B** **C2** **C**

High and lifted up,   Jesus, Son of God,

    D   **D/C**   **G/B** **C** **Dsus**

The Darling of heaven, cruci- fied.

      Am7   **G/B** **C**

Worthy is the Lamb,

      Am7   **G/B** **Dsus**

Worthy is the Lamb.

Tag   **Am7**   **G/B** **C**

Worthy is the Lamb,

      Am7   **G/B** **Dsus**

Worthy is the Lamb,

      Am7   **G/B** **Dsus** **D** **G**

Worthy is the Lamb.

You Are Good

Words and Music by
ISRAEL HOUGHTON

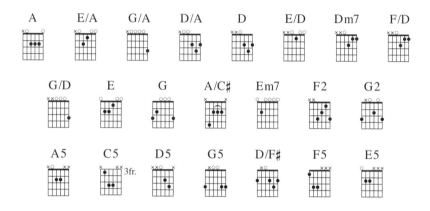

Verse

A
Lord, You are good
　　　　　　E/A　　　　　　　　**G/A D/A**
And Your mercy endureth forever.
A　　　　　　　　　　**E/A**　　　　　**G/A D/A**
Lord, You are good and Your mercy endureth forever.
D　　　　　**E/D**
People from every nation and tongue,
Dm7　　　　　　**F/D G/D**
From generation to gen-　eration.

Chorus   A   E   G   D

We worship You. Hallelujah! Hallelujah!

        A   E   G   D

We worship You for who You are.

        A   E   G   D

We worship You. Hallelujah! Hallelujah!

        A/C♯   Em7   F2   G2

We worship You for who You are,

              A

And You are good.

Interlude   A5   C5   D5

                         Yes, You are, yes, You are, yes, You are!

A5   G5   D/F♯   F5   E5

        So good, so good!

Bridge   F5   E5   A5   C5   D5

You are good,   all the time.

                 A5   C5   D5

All the time,   You are good.

You Are Holy
(Prince of Peace)

Words and Music by
MARK IMBODEN
and TAMMI RHOTON

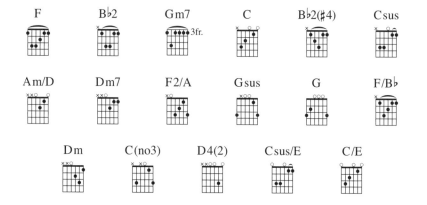

Verse
*(Ladies echo
Men's part)*

        F   **B♭2**
You are holy. You are mighty.

        Gm7   **C**
You are worthy, worthy of praise.

        F   **B♭2**   **Gm7**
I will follow; I will listen; I will love You

C   **F**   **C**   **F**
All of my days. (all of my days.)

Chorus
*(Ladies sing
lyrics in italics)*

     B♭2(♯4) **B♭2**   **C** **Csus**
I will sing to and wor- ship
You are Lord of lords, You are King of kings,

     Am/D **Dm7** **F2/A**
The King who is wor- thy.
You are mighty God, Lord of everything.

      B♭2(♯4) **B♭2**   **C** **Csus**
And I will love and a-   dore Him,
You're Em-manu- el, You're the Great I AM,

      Am/D **Dm7** **F2/A**
And I will bow down be- fore Him.
You're the Prince of Peace who is the Lamb.

      B♭2(♯4) **B♭2**   **C** **Csus**
And I will sing to and   wor- ship
You're the Living God, You're my saving grace.

   Am/D **Dm7**   **F2/A**
The King who is wor- thy.
You will reign forever, You are Ancient of Days.

     B♭2(♯4) **B♭2** **C** **Csus**
And I will love and a- dore Him,
You are Alpha, Omega, Beginning and End.

     Am/D **Dm7** **Gsus** **G**
And I will bow down be- fore   Him.
You're my Savior, Messiah, Redeemer and Friend.

    B♭2
You're my Prince of Peace,

    C   **F** **(F/B♭** **Csus** **C)**
And I will live my life for You.

Tag **Dm**   **B♭2**
    You're my Prince of Peace,
    C(no3)
And I will live my life for You.
D4(2) **Dm** **Csus/E** **C/E** **B♭2** **B♭2(♯4)** **B♭2** **(F)**
Oh,   oh,   oh.

You Are My All in All

Words and Music by
DENNIS L. JERNIGAN

Melody:

You are my strength when I am weak,

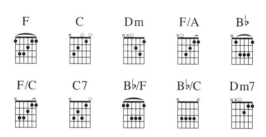

F   C   Dm   F/A   B♭

F/C   C7   B♭/F   B♭/C   Dm7

Verse 1

        F   C   Dm

You are my strength when I am weak,

           F/A   B♭

You are the treasure that I seek;

           F/C   C   F   C7

You are my all   in   all.

      F   C   Dm

Seeking You as a precious jewel,

           F/A   B♭

Lord, to give up, I'd be a fool;

           F/C   C   B♭/F   F   B♭/C

You are my all   in   all.

Chorus   F   C   Dm7   F/A   B♭   F/C   C   F   C7
Je- sus, Lamb of God,   Worthy is   Your name!
         F   C   Dm7   F/A   B♭   F/C   C   B♭/F   F
Je- sus, Lamb of God,   Worthy is   Your name!

Verse 2   F   C   Dm
         Taking my sin, my cross, my shame,
               F/A   B♭
         Rising again I bless Your name;
                  F/C   C   F   C7
         You are my all   in   all.
         F   C   Dm
         When I fall down, You pick me up;
               F/A   B♭
         When I am dry, You fill my cup;
                  F/C   C   B♭/F   F   B♭/C
         You are my all   in   all.

We Fall Down

Words and Music by
CHRIS TOMLIN

Melody:

We fall___ down,___

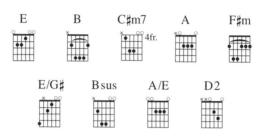

Chorus

    E   B   C♯m7   A   F♯m
We fall down, we lay our crowns at the feet of Jesus,

    E   B   C♯m7   A   B
The greatness of mercy and love at the feet of Jesus.

       E/G♯ A   E/G♯ F♯m
And we cry holy, holy,   holy,

       E/G♯ A   E/G♯ F♯m
And we cry holy, holy,   holy,

       C♯m7 B A   E/G♯ F♯m
And we   cry holy, holy, holy

Bsus   B   E A/E E D2 (E)
Is   the Lamb.

You Are My King
(Amazing Love)

Words and Music by
BILLY FOOTE

Melody:

I'm for-giv - en

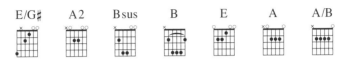

E/G♯   A2   Bsus   B   E   A   A/B

Verse

E/G♯   A2   Bsus   B
    I'm forgiven because You were forsaken.

E/G♯   A2   Bsus   B
    I'm accepted;   You were condemned.

E/G♯   A2   Bsus   B
    I'm alive and well, Your Spirit is within me

A2   B   E
Because You died and rose again.

Chorus

E   A
    Amazing love, how can it be

E   Bsus   B   A/B
    That You, my King, would die for me?

E   A
    Amazing love, I know it's true;

E   Bsus   B   (A/B)
    It's my joy to honor You.

A   B   E
In all I do   I honor You.

Bridge

E
You are my King, You are my King.

Jesus, You are my King. Jesus, You are my King.

You're Worthy of My Praise

Words and Music by
DAVID RUIS

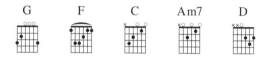

Verse 1 **G**

I will worship (I will worship)

    F

With all of my heart (with all of my heart).

C

I will praise You (I will praise You)

    G   **Am7** **D**

With all of my strength (all of   my strength).

G

I will seek You (I will seek You)

F

All of my days (all of my days).

C   **G**   **Am7**   **D**

I will follow (I will follow) all of Your ways (all Your ways).

GUITAR CHORD SONGBOOK

Chorus   **G**   **D**

       I will give You all my worship,

      C   **Am7**   **D**

       I will give You all my praise.

      G   **D**

       You alone I long to worship,

      C   **Am7**   **D**   **G**

       You alone are worthy of my praise.

Verse 2   **G**

      I will bow down (I will bow down)

         F

      And hail You as King (and hail You as King).

      C

      I will serve You (I will serve),

            G   **Am7**   **D**

      Give You everything (give You everything).

      G

      I will lift up (I will lift up)

         F

      My eyes to Your throne (my eyes to Your throne).

      C

      I will trust You (I will trust You),

      G   **Am7**   **D**

      Trust You alone (trust You alone).

Your Love, Oh Lord

Words and Music by
MAC POWELL, BRAD AVERY,
TAI ANDERSON and DAVID CARR

Melody:

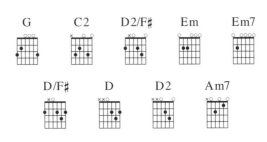

Chorus

| G | C2 | G | D2/F♯ |

Your love, oh Lord,   reaches to the heavens.

| Em | C2 | G | D2/F♯ |

Your faithfulness   stretches to the sky.

| Em7 | C2 | G | D/F♯ |

Your righteousness is like the mighty mountains.

| Em | C2 | G | D |

Your justice flows like the ocean's tide.

Verse

| D2 | C2 | G |

I will lift my   voice to worship You, my King.

| D2 | C2 | Am7 | D |

I will find my   strength in the shadow of Your wings.

Tag

| G | C2 | G | D/F♯ |

Your love, oh Lord,   reaches to the heavens.

| Em | C2 | G |

Your faithfulness   stretches to the sky.

A

Above All--2
Agnus Dei--10
Alive, Forever, Amen--4
Ancient of Days---6
As the Deer--8
Awesome God---11
Awesome in This Place--12

B

Be Glorified--13
Be Unto Your Name--14
Beautiful One--20
Better Is One Day---16
Blessed Be Your Name--18
Breathe---21

C

Change My Heart, O God--24
Come Just As You Are---22
Come, Now Is the Time to Worship---------------------------------25
Cry of My Heart--28

D

Days of Elijah--26
Draw Me Close---29

E

Enough--30
Every Move I Make--36
Everyday--32
Everyone Arise---34

F

Famous One---37
Forever---38
Friend of God---40

G

Give Thanks--41
God of Wonders---42
Grace Flows Down--46
Great Is the Lord--44

H

Hallelujah (Your Love Is Amazing)--------------------------------------47
He Has Made Me Glad (I Will Enter His Gates)-------------------------48
He Is Exalted--49
He Knows My Name--54
Hear Our Praises---50
Here I Am to Worship--52
Holy and Anointed One---55
Holy Is the Lord--56
How Deep the Father's Love for Us------------------------------------58
How Great Is Our God--62
How Great Thou Art---60
Hunger and Thirst---63
Hungry (Falling on My Knees)--64

I

I Could Sing of Your Love Forever---------------------------------------65
I Give You My Heart--66
I Love You, Lord---67
I Stand in Awe--68
I Want to Know You (In the Secret)--------------------------------------70
I Will Call Upon the Lord---72
I Worship You, Almighty God---73
In Christ Alone--74
Indescribable---76

J

Jesus, Name Above All Names---84

K

King of Glory---78
Knowing You (All I Once Held Dear)-------------------------------------80

L

Let Everything That Has Breath---82
Let It Rise--85
Let My Words Be Few (I'll Stand in Awe of You)-------------------------86
Lord, I Lift Your Name on High---87
Lord, Reign in Me--88

M

Majesty---90
Meet with Me---92
More Love, More Power---93
More Precious Than Silver--104
My Redeemer Lives---94

N

No Other Gods--96

O

O Praise Him (All This for a King)-------------------------------------98
Once Again---100
Only a God Like You--102
Open Our Eyes--105
Open the Eyes of My Heart---106

R

Refiner's Fire--107
Rock of Ages---108

S

Sanctuary--109

Shine, Jesus, Shine--110

Shout to the Lord--112

Shout to the North---114

Sing to the King--116

Sometimes by Step--118

Step by Step--120

T

Take My Life---121

That's Why We Praise Him---122

The Heart of Worship---124

The Potter's Hand---126

The Power of Your Love---128

The Wonderful Cross--130

There Is None Like You--136

Trading My Sorrows--132

W

We Bow Down---134

We Bring the Sacrifice of Praise----------------------------------137

We Fall Down--150

We Want to See Jesus Lifted High-------------------------------138

We Will Glorify---140

Worthy Is the Lamb--142

Y

You Are Good--144

You Are Holy (Prince of Peace)----------------------------------146

You Are My All in All--148

You Are My King (Amazing Love)-------------------------------151

You're Worthy of My Praise---------------------------------------152

Your Love, Oh Lord---154

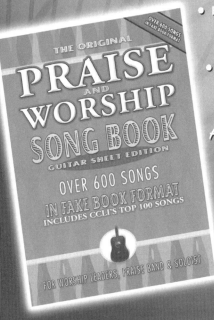